INSTITUTIONALIZING EXPERT SYSTEMS

A Handbook for Managers

Jay Liebowitz, D.Sc.

Department of Management Science
George Washington University

Prentice Hall
Englewood Cliffs, New Jersey 07632

Library of Congress Cataloging-in-Publication Data

Liebowitz, Jay.
    Institutionalizing expert systems : a handbook for managers / Jay
Liebowitz.
        p.   cm.
    Includes bibliographical references and index.
    ISBN 0-13-472077-6
    1. Expert systems (Computer science)   I. Title.
QA76.76.E95L53   1991
658'.05633--dc20   90-37629
                                                            CIP

Editorial/production supervision
  and interior design: Harriet Tellem
Cover design: Lundgren Graphics
Manufacturing buyers: Kelly Behr/Susan Brunke

**Dedicated to
Janet, Jason, and Kenneth**

The publisher offers discounts on this book when ordered
in bulk quantities. For more information, write:
    Special Sales/College Marketing
    Prentice-Hall, Inc.
    College Technical and Reference Division
    Englewood Cliffs, NJ 07632

Printed in the United States of America
10 9 8 7 6 5 4 3 2 1

ISBN 0-13-472077-6

Prentice-Hall International (UK) Limited, *London*
Prentice-Hall of Australia Pty. Limited, *Sydney*
Prentice-Hall Canada Inc., *Toronto*
Prentice-Hall Hispanoamericana, S.A., *Mexico*
Prentice-Hall of India Private Limited, *New Delhi*
Prentice-Hall of Japan, Inc., *Tokyo*
Simon & Schuster Asia Pte. Ltd., *Singapore*
Editora Prentice-Hall do Brasil, Ltda., *Rio de Janeiro*

CONTENTS

PREFACE

Expert systems are becoming an important part of today's information technology. Expert systems are being used more and more in our lives, as evidenced by the Federal Aviation Administration's approval to have expert systems in use at 400 airports in order to check for explosives in passengers' baggage. Other examples of expert systems being used on a daily basis include expert systems for computer configuration, fault isolation and diagnosis, network management, health insurance claims processing, loan approvals, and many other applications.

However, there are still many expert systems that, once built, never are "transitioned" into an organization and thus are not used. One of the major problems preventing widespread use of expert systems is the poor "institutionalization" process of expert systems. An expert system may be accurate and well designed, but if proper implementation, transitioning, and maintenance are lacking, then the expert system will not be used and the project might be thought of as a failure.

This book addresses this glaring need to make managers, as well as knowledge engineers, aware of this expert system institutionalization problem. This book serves as a quick guide to help transition expert systems into the organization. Specifically, the book looks at the following: an awareness of expert systems for managers, user training strategies, user support services strategies, maintenance guidelines, documentation guidelines, and legal issues, all relating to expert systems. Some case studies are used throughout the book to provide a further opportunity for understanding expert system development and institutionalization issues.

I thank Paul Becker, Noreen Regina, Harriet Tellem, the Prentice Hall staff, the reviewers, and my colleagues for their help in the development of this book. I also gratefully acknowledge the help of my wife, Janet, who encouraged me to write this book. I hope you enjoy the book!

. . . Jay Liebowitz, D.Sc.

PART I

Setting the Stage
and Looking Beyond

CHAPTER 1

EXPERT SYSTEMS: NEAR- AND LONG-TERM FORECASTS

Even though it has only been since about 1980 that the commercialization of expert systems began, expert systems already are making their way into the mainstream of numerous industries. According to Feigenbaum et al. [1], there are already about 2,000 expert systems being used worldwide and approximately 10,000 expert systems are being either developed and/or field tested. This growth in expert systems applications seems consistent with the increase in funds put into the expert systems market. According to *AI Trends '88* [2], the U.S. market for expert systems has grown from $4 million in 1981 to $400 million in 1988, and is projected to increase to well over $800 million in the 1990s.

Before we discuss strategies for implementing expert systems in an organization, which is the focus of this book, we will first look at why expert systems are important and where they are expected to head in the coming years.

Already, there are many payoffs from expert systems [3]. Texas Instruments' capital-proposal package expert system speeds the process of developing capital proposals by 20 times. This reduces cost overruns and preparation expenses by an average of $2 million a year. American Express's Authorizer's Assistant increases the efficiency of its credit authorizers by 45% to 67%. Du Pont has had a return on investment in expert systems through 1987 of 1,500% and an aggregate savings of $10 million. Digital Equipment Corporation (DEC) believes it is saving $70 million a year from the 10 major expert systems it uses. According to *High Technology Business,* half of the Fortune 500 companies are now investing in the development and maintenance of expert systems. Expert systems are even being used by retail stores, such as the Los Angeles department store chain of Carter Hawley Hall Stores; Carter Hawley officials found that sales improved 5% in stores that used the technology [4].

Why are expert systems gaining so much popularity? There are several reasons. First, expert systems allow organizations to preserve or document knowledge before an expert leaves the company or retires [5]. In this manner, expert systems help in building the corporate memory of the firm. Second, worker productivity can increase with expert systems. Third, expert systems allow the proliferation of a consistently high level of expertise at a number of sites, thus enhancing distribution of the knowledge of the expert(s). Fourth, expert systems can give experts the opportunity to pursue other areas of professional interest that they otherwise would not have had the time to pursue. Fifth, expert systems can facilitate training of new employees in selected areas. Sixth, expert systems can be used as a second opinion to test the soundness of one's decisions. Seventh, expert systems can be used to gain an edge on a company's competitors. Last, expert systems provide a logical, systematic way of stepping the user through solving a problem, particularly helpful under time and pressure constraints.

Badiru [17] believes that the key to successful development and implementation of an expert system is the Triple C principle of communication, cooperation, and coordination. These three components are important in emphasizing the management aspects of building expert systems. Explicitly or implicitly, the success or failure of any project depends on the prevailing levels of these three components [17].

Badiru [17] believes that there are ten major items that constitute the life cycle of a typical expert system project. These guidelines, in order, are as follows [17]:

1. Definition of Problem Area
   a. Define problem domain using keywords that signify the importance of the problem to the overall organization.
   b. Locate domain expert willing to contribute expertise to the knowledge base.
   c. Prepare and announce the development plan.
2. Personnel Assignment
   a. The project group and the respective tasks should be announced.
   b. A qualified project manager should be appointed.
   c. A solid line of command should be established and enforced.
3. Project Initiation
   a. Arrange organizational meeting.
   b. Discuss general approach to the problem.
   c. Prepare specific development plan.
   d. Arrange for the installation of needed hardware and tools.
4. System Prototype
   a. Develop a prototype system.
   b. Test an initial implementation.
   c. Learn more about problem area from test results.
5. Full System Development
   a. Expand the prototype knowledge base.
   b. Evaluate the user interface structure.
   c. Incorporate user training facilities and documentation.
6. System Verification
   a. Get experts and potential users involved.
   b. Ensure that the system performs as designed.
   c. Debug the system as needed.
7. System Validation
   a. Ensure that the system yields expected outputs.
   b. Validation can take the form of:
      • Evaluating performance level (e.g., percentage of success in so many trials).
      • Measuring level of deviation from expected outputs.

- Measuring the effectiveness of the system output in solving the problem under consideration.

8. System Integration.
   a. Implement the full system as planned.
   b. Ensure the system can coexist with systems already in operation.
   c. Arrange for technology transfer to other projects.
9. System Maintenance.
   a. Arrange for continuing maintenance of the system.
   b. Update knowledge base as new pieces of information become available.
   c. Retain responsibility for system performance or delegate to well-trained and authorized personnel.
10. Documentation
    a. Prepare full documentation of system.
    b. Prepare user's guide.
    c. Appoint a user consultant.

It is no wonder that expert systems are becoming increasingly used in organizations. But what lies ahead in the near term—say two years from now? The rest of this chapter will look at possible trends in expert system technology and applications in the next two years, and then will make some long-term forecasts. These trends are presented early in this book in order to give the manager a good sense of the current and future expert systems market.

EXPERT SYSTEM TRENDS IN THE NEAR TERM

There are several current trends in expert systems that are taking shape. These can be categorized as towards: (1) integration, (2) mass-market applications, and (3) organizational adoption of expert systems. Each of these areas will be discussed in turn.

Integration of Expert Systems with Traditional Technology

One major trend in the expert systems field is the integration of expert systems and AI technology with "traditional" data processing technology. To maximize the usefulness of expert systems in organizations, companies are linking expert systems with existing databases. Standalone expert systems are still prevalent, but most of the expert systems being developed today, and in the near term, are being integrated with existing databases and management information systems (MIS). Part of this push is because MIS departments are starting to promote and support expert systems technology.

Ed Feigenbaum believes that

> Up to now the expert systems have tended to be pushed by the end users—the engineers or the managers. Now the MIS (Management Information Systems) people can be involved and can be pushing these applications. In Japan, interestingly, it has always been the MIS people who have been pushing the technologies. They just extend their sort of job shop programming and add expert systems to it. [18]

Harry Reinstein, Chief Executive Officer of Aion Corporation, has similar thoughts. He states:

> The major trend that we have seen over the past two or three years has been away from a focus on rare and exotic expert system applications and towards the application of inference-based technology to the extension of, or building of, more traditional applications. There is a demonstrable economic value in building an application using the inference-based approach. This approach is well suited for the logically complex rapidly changing application, which represents the challenge that data processing departments are facing. Currently DP (Data Processing)/MIS needs to step up to the issues of building software applications that make their companies more competitive, more effective, and more efficient. The shift away from the expert system orientation and towards the data processing orientation is perhaps the major initiative of the future. [19]

An example of this integration is shown in AI Corporation's KBMS expert system development tool. It connects with DB2 databases and incorporates Intellect's natural language features. Information Builders Inc. allows their Level 5 expert system shell to be linked with their FOCUS database management systems. One important trend resulting from this expert systems integration with mainframe database management systems is the consequent interest generated in developing expert systems and shells for IBM mainframes, which is useful because many organizations use an IBM mainframe environment. In the near term, more expert system shells will be developed for the IBM mainframe. Already, examples of shells that exist for the IBM mainframe include: AI Corporation's KBMS, Aion Corporation's ADS, Intellicorp's KEE, and IBM's ESE and KnowledgeTool.

The integration of expert systems with existing databases is already fairly commonplace. This is particularly evident in expert systems used in the telecommunications environment [6]. ACE, developed by Bell Labs, and COMPASS, developed by GTE Labs, are two examples of operational expert systems used daily for fault isolation and diagnosis of telecommunications switches and lines. CRAS, the data management and report generation system, is a central part of ACE's operations. CRAS supplies the data to ACE on which to operate. When projecting into the 1990s during the Space Station era, the need to couple databases with expert systems—especially real-time expert systems—technology will become ever more apparent and demanding.

With the realization that expert systems will be integrated with database management systems, large database companies will purchase some expert system companies. Information Builders Inc. is an example of this phenomenon. More generalized computer firms, as opposed to specialized expert system/AI companies, will become major players in the expert systems market in the coming years. IBM, DEC, and TI are already very involved in expert systems technology. Apple, which acquired Coral Software, is also getting involved in the Lisp/expert systems market. Expert systems will be integrated not only with database management systems but also with CAD/CAM technology. A prime example of this is American Cimflex, a CAD/CAM firm, merging with Teknowledge, an expert systems firm. American Cimflex wants to use knowledge-based systems technology with CAD/CAM. With such mergers and acquisitions taking place within the computer industry, existing expert systems firms like Teknowledge, The Carnegie Group, Intellicorp, and Inference Corporation will start to feel pressure from the IBMs, DECs, Apples, and TIs. Hence, in the coming years, only the "fittest" will likely survive, as many specialized expert systems companies are weeded out by the larger "all purpose" computer firms.

Mass-Market Expert System Applications

Another major trend that will develop in the coming years is the targeting of expert systems for the mass market. There will be a major push to use expert systems for a large target market: namely, the layperson, consumer, or parent. Already, several of these mass-market expert systems have been developed. "Ask Dan" (now called "Tax Cut") is an expert system developed for providing tax advice for the layperson. EXSAMPLE is an expert system designed for determining which is the appropriate statistical analysis to be used for a given purpose; it is linked with various PC-based statistical packages like SPSS and SAS. Family Care Software has developed an expert system to provide medical advice on children's health problems. STS/Expert is an expert system geared towards helping consumers trade in the stock market.

In the near term, more of these mass-marketed expert systems will be developed and sold to the public for a reasonable price— perhaps $49 to $125. An important anticipated result from the use of these expert systems by the everyday individual might be an increase in the number of lawsuits associated with expert systems. Currently, there have only been a few. One case involved an expert whose knowledge was used to develop an expert system. The expert was fired after the expert system was already being marketed commercially. The expert sued the company in order to obtain royalties for the use of his knowledge in the commercially sold expert system. More lawsuits will probably result from the use, nonuse, and misuse of expert systems in the future [7].

More Organizations Will Adopt Expert Systems in Their Business Practices

In the near term, more organizations will learn about, experiment with, and develop and use expert systems in their business practices. Already, about half of the Fortune 500 companies are developing and using expert systems, and this trend will continue. The use of hypertext, CD-ROM technology, and neural networks will play a role in enhancing expert system applications in the near term. Additionally, more powerful and sophisticated expert system shells will be developed for the 386 microcomputers; KEE and ART-IM are now available. This will further the availability and usage of expert systems in organizations. In the near term, there will be domain-specific shells developed, such as for scheduling and for planning. Shells will be developed for a particular functional area, and thus will become more specialized. Additionally, more expert system shells will be developed for the Macintosh computer. Currently, very few expert system shells exist on the Mac, such as Nexpert Object by Neuron Data. Part of this future push will come from Apple, which is just getting involved in AI technology. To further promote expert systems technology within an organization, more business- and managerial-oriented expert system conferences and literature will result [8,9].

Other Near-Term Expert Systems Trends

Besides those already mentioned, there will be several other trends taking shape in the coming years. These include [11–15]:

- More automated knowledge acquisition tools developed.
- More centers for Artificial Intelligence formed in universities, industry, and government.
- More techniques, paradigms, and tools developed for handling distributed AI problems, such as in telecommunications.
- More real-time expert systems and associated shells developed.
- More structured techniques and methodologies developed and used for expert system building [10].
- Better ways for tailoring explanations depending upon the type of user—knowledge engineer, expert, novice user, and knowledgeable user.
- More research in incorporating learning into expert systems.
- More work in coupling together expert systems, database management systems, and natural language understanding.
- More applications integrating expert systems with hyper-media/hypertext.
- Increasing application of expert systems and knowledge system products which enhance the value of existing applications (payroll, inventory, personnel, and so on) rather than simply the purchase of standalone expert system shells.

- Increasing number of neural networks applications.
- Rapidly growing number of real, operational expert system applications.
- More realistic marketing focus on the products with the most long-term potential.
- Many vendors positioning their AI products as practical software development tools, offering direct advantages in terms of productivity and speed of development.

Even though the next few years for expert systems are relatively bright, there are still some negative factors that need to be considered. These include [13]:

- Too many projects still end in failure—in the sense that they do not produce an operational system of value.
- Although the technology is beginning to settle down, there is still too much instability in key areas, such as interfaces and data exchange standards.

In spite of these potential negative factors, the near term forecast of the expert systems market remains bright. Herb Schorr [14] indicates that by the early 1990s, expert systems will be returning about $115.5 million per year on their investment, based on projects with approximately 10-to-1 payback ratios.

LONG SHOTS

Looking a decade ahead, there are some "long shot" AI/expert system trends that could possibly emerge. These include [16]:

- Corporations may embrace AI technology as the cure to many problems. Every major corporation may use some form of AI/expert systems technology.
- Since almost all corporate managers will likely have AI capabilities at their disposal at the touch of their fingertips, the knowledge engineer's position, as we know it today, may be in jeopardy.

- Companies may allocate large portions of their budgets to the building or application of AI products and services.
- Lisp and Prolog will probably become almost obsolete for commercial AI applications, in favor of using conventional programming languages like C.
- Most expert systems will likely have built-in learning capabilities.

CONCLUSIONS

The years ahead in this age of artificial intelligence look exciting and promising. The developers of expert systems technology and applications should be careful not to create overoptimistic or false expectations of what AI can deliver. With expert systems and AI brought into proper focus, organizations will be able to consider AI technology as one of the tools in their toolkit.

REFERENCES

[1]   Feigenbaum, E., P. McCorduck, and H.P. Nii, *The Rise of the Expert Company*, Times Books, 1988.

[2]   DM Data, Inc., *AI Trends '88*, Albuquerque, New Mexico, 1988.

[3]   Enslow, B, "The Payoff from Expert Systems," *Across the Board*, January/February 1989.

[4]   "Retailers Take to High Technology as the Pace of Competition Grows," *The Washington Post*, February 12, 1989, pp. H1, H5.

[5]   Liebowitz, J., *Introduction to Expert Systems*, Mitchell Publishing, Watsonville, CA, 1988.

[6]   Liebowitz, J. (ed.), *Expert System Applications to Telecommunications*, John Wiley, New York, 1988.

[7]   Zeide, J.S. and J. Liebowitz, "Using Expert Systems: The Legal Perspective," *IEEE Expert*, Los Alamitos, CA, Spring 1987.

[8]   DeSalvo, D.A. and J. Liebowitz (eds.), *Managing AI and Expert Systems*, Prentice Hall, Englewood Cliffs, NJ, 1990.

[9]   Liebowitz, J. (ed.), *Expert Systems for Business and Management*, Prentice Hall, Englewood Cliffs, NJ, 1990.

[10]   Liebowitz, J. and D.A. DeSalvo (eds.), *Structuring Expert Systems: Domain, Design, and Development*, Yourdon Press/Prentice Hall, Englewood Cliffs, NJ, 1989.

[11]   Liebowitz, J., "Expert Systems: The Near Term Forecast," *Proceedings of the International Conference on Expert System Applications*, IITT-International, Paris, October 1989.

[12]   Newquist, H.P., "Welcome to 1989, The Beginning of the End of the Decade," *AI Trends*, Vol. 5, No. 4, The Relayer Group, Scottsdale, Arizona, January 1989.

[13]   Johnson, T., J. Hewett, C. Guilfoyle, and J. Jeffcoate, "Expert Systems—The Second Wave," *The Knowledge Engineering Review*, Cambridge University Press, 1988.

[14]   Chapnick, P., "Real People, Real Applications," *AI Expert*, Miller Freeman Publications, San Francisco, CA, June 1989.

[15]   Monger, R.F., "AI Applications: What's Their Competitive Potential?", *Journal of Information Systems Management*, Auerbach Publishers, New York, Vol. 5, No. 3, Summer 1988.

[16]   Liebowitz, J., "Artificial Intelligence and the Corporate Environment," *Information Executive*, Vol. 2, No. 1, Data Processing Management Association, Park Ridge, Illinois, Winter 1989.

[17]   Badiru, A.B., "Successful Initiation of Expert Systems Projects," IEEE Transactions on Engineering Management, Vol. 35, No. 3, IEEE, August 1988.

[18]   Owen, K., "Interview with Edward Feigenbaum," Expert Systems, Learned Information, Oxford, England, Vol. 6, No. 2, April 1989.

[19]   Interview with Harry C. Reinstein, SIG-AI Newsletter, Data Processing Management Association, Worcester, MA, Vol. 1, No. 3, May 1989.

PART II

Selling Management on Expert Systems

CHAPTER 2

CREATING MANAGEMENT AWARENESS OF EXPERT SYSTEMS

To succeed, a company expert systems project must have the involvement and backing of management. There is a need for a project champion—typically someone in top management. But before you can recruit a manager to champion your cause, you must first build a foundation of awareness in your organization. According to a Price Waterhouse survey of information technology executives, the top problem preventing widespread use of expert systems is the lack of management awareness regarding expert systems. You must help management understand that expert systems are a new technology that can help them meet their strategic goals. In the expert systems environment, there are several ways to arouse the interest and curiosity of management in order to gain their winning support. This chapter will address these ways for creating an awareness of expert systems among management within the organization.

APPROACH 1: ADDRESS A PROBLEM WHICH NEEDS A BETTER SOLUTION AND USE PROTOTYPING

Leonard-Barton [1] believes that when introducing a new technology one needs to use an "integrative innovation" approach. Leonard-Barton believes that adopting an integrative approach can increase the chances of success for the project. Integrative innovation requires attention to three management domains at once [1]:

- Cultivating users as codevelopers.
- Creating a support system, including a network of supporters and an adequate delivery system for users.
- Organizational prototyping (i.e., experimentation and planned learning about the integration of the new solution).

A corollary to this first approach is the technique of developing an expert system prototype to show management the feasibility of applying expert systems technology to their problem. In fact, one of the best ways, according to managers, to make managers aware of expert systems and then have them sponsor the project is to develop an expert system prototype, usually by someone in-house. If someone does this on his/her own initiative, then this demonstration prototype might be enough to spark the interest of management and have the expert system developed more fully. The demonstration of the expert system prototype can show management the capabilities of expert systems and alert managers to their potential, as well as their limitations.

To help build this prototype, an expert system shell is typically used for speeding up the development process. Harry Reinstein, in talking about his company's (Aion Corporation) ADS expert system shell, states that [8]:

> The most common justification for acquiring our product is the productivity gained in the development process. We're seeing about a ten times improvement in calendar time and resource utilization. We're also seeing earlier and more intimate involvement of the end user application specialist, who has become a more participative and effective member of the development team. That not only improves the quality of the application, but

improves the timing and the productivity allowing the application to meet the end user requirements. There's also an increase in productivity in the delivery process. People can develop on one platform and deliver in another.

CASE STUDY: The AI Lab in the Internal Revenue Service*

Tom Beckman describes how an awareness for expert systems and artificial intelligence was created within the Internal Revenue Service (IRS) and how the IRS's/AI Lab developed [5]:

In 1983, staff of then Assistant Commissioner for Planning, Finance and Research, John Wedick, conducted a study that indicated that AI technology might be profitably applied to tasks in the IRS. In 1984, in response to this study, Wedick created the IRS AI program. Prior to the AI program, the IRS did not possess any capability to develop AI applications in-house, nor did it feel competent even to contract work out to AI vendors.

Wedick's staff interviewed leading academic researchers and business practitioners to find the best methods of achieving an AI capability within the IRS. As a result, Wedick devised a program with two training strategies to train IRS domain experts in AI technology. A one-year program was designed to develop AI project managers capable of overseeing vendor work and evaluating contract proposals for AI services. Four program participants were trained in project management and design at a leading research concern. A two-year course of study was designed to educate domain experts in AI techniques and create a cadre capable of developing extensive AI applications in-house. Eight two-year participants were schooled at one of the three leading AI universities.

In 1985, Wedick created the AI Lab, a section within the Research Division, one of many functions under Wedick. The Lab is currently staffed with 22 AI Specialists. Thus far, two classes have completed the AI training program. A third class began in Fall 1989. Prior to receiving the AI training, most of the staff were domain experts from various functional areas within IRS. The remainder were computer programmers and systems analysts from Computer Services.

*T.J. Beckman, "An Expert System in Taxation," in *Expert Systems for Business and Management*, J. Liebowitz (ed.), 1990, 43–44. Reprinted by permission of Prentice Hall, Inc., Englewood Cliffs, New Jersey.

John Wedick, now one of two Deputy Commissioners, has provided continuing support for the AI Lab, ensuring its long-term viability. Not only has he funded subsequent classes of trainees, but also equipment and software procured for the Lab have provided a work environment that has encouraged a host of AI applications. In contrast with the concentrated effort of an entire staff working on one project, the AI Lab has 18 ongoing projects, most of them with only one Specialist assigned. In addition, there are several student projects that in the future may become permanent projects.

Because expert systems technology is most effective only on certain classes of problems or tasks, only trained AI Specialists are qualified to select the most promising projects. Hence, in many cases, AI Lab participants have had complete freedom in selecting projects. However, on some projects this freedom has created its own drawbacks. Support and participation by the function with the selected project has often been disinterested at best until a successful prototype has been built and demonstrated. Freedom in project selection as well as diversity in domain expertise has resulted in various AI applications under development.

CASE STUDY: Blue Cross of Western Pennsylvania (BCWP)*

David Gorney describes how management support was obtained for expert systems work at Blue Cross of Western Pennsylvania [6]:

> Corporate management was receptive toward a plan to conduct a small research project with the goal of identifying payback ideas. The use of internal staff was out of the question as BCWP was in the process of laying the groundwork for a major new development project using relational database technology. In this case, outside consulting was the answer. The outside consultant that I had met at the security meeting was brought on board to assist in the effort to determine the best business problem to target. During a four-month span of very intensive work, two prototype systems were developed.

*D.J. Gorney, "Expert Systems in Health Insurance," in *Expert Systems for Business and Management*, J. Liebowitz (ed.), 1990, 173–174. Reprinted by permission of Prentice Hall, Inc., Englewood Cliffs, New Jersey.

The process of getting started was memorable for several reasons. Up to that time, my entire career (originating at Rockwell in 1971 in a typical IBM shop) had consisted of mainframe problems and mainframe type systems resolutions. I quickly learned that personal computers should not be underestimated as development tools. In a short span of time, I was using dBase III, Kermit, Prolog, and of course, the MS-DOS operating system. I could see that word processing packages and productivity tools like SideKick for calendaring, memos, and project management certainly opened some new ways of thinking.

In retrospect, what may have changed the most was my perception about the way work is conducted in the conventional large information services setting.

As a manager, constant telephone calls, meetings, and interruptions become the normal diet in the office. The only solution was to allocate evening and weekend time for the prototype development. This project taught me a lot about reserving time to be productive, and, as the results started to appear, to have fun. In my opinion, companies need to encourage employees to be creative and enjoy their work, sometimes at the expense of rigid and traditional personnel policies. More often than not, BCWP has been the progressive environment that is needed for innovation. There can be no doubt that one can be much more productive at work if that endeavor is self-motivated. To put it simply, this new expert system development work was fun.

However, those days were not all fun. As can be expected, many in the organization did not know of or understand the project, or were openly resentful about it. Curiously enough, the most notable resistance came from the management of the system development group. I had proposed that this area should become involved with the project to share in the learning process. After a period of reluctant participation, system management finally conceded that the expert systems were here to stay. It's curious how politics, turf issues, and perhaps even jealousy work to hinder new ideas. Most ironic is the situation when these attitudes surface in the change agents of the corporation, the system developers themselves.

Having been through numerous development projects, I long ago learned to cope with these problems and move ahead concentrating on the positive. I also learned that new ideas are often squelched if someone in the senior executive ranks is not a proponent, and that is really as it should be. We were fortunate enough to have a proponent in our organization, Mr. Robert Schuler, now the Executive Vice President and Chief Operating Officer of BCWP, who was then the Senior Vice President of Finance and Information Services. Without his support, the budding expert system projects at BCWP were doomed to oblivion.

One of the initial prototypes was the MAC (Marketing Account Consultant) Expert System. The premise behind the MAC Expert System was to gather critical information about one specific large corporate client customer into a knowledge base which would then serve to assist the marketing account executive in servicing and selling to that client. Information was to be fed into the MAC from corporate subject databases (Provider or Hospital, Customer, Claim, and Subscriber) in addition to financial and accounting databases. The online public Dow Jones and information retrieval resources were also part of the MAC system.

The bottom line of this project was to provide marketing with a tool to help manage accounts and anticipate problems and requests. Perhaps a bit too abstract for its time, MAC was placed on hold, yet may be reactivated in the future.

At the conclusion of the research contract, it was decided to shift gears in a sense and begin to bring the process of developing expert systems in-house. Budget funds were approved to make expert systems a reality within BCWP.

After a briefing session with senior management, where two project ideas and prototypes were demonstrated, the go-ahead was received to begin development of the IPDR (Inter Plan Data Reporting) Error Analysis Expert System, later to become known as the PlanTracker. The PlanTracker was chosen as our first project because it offered the possibility of favorably impacting the cash flow process that occurs between all Blue Cross plans, other plans, and ultimately customers.

APPROACH 2: BE INVENTIVE IN AROUSING MANAGEMENT'S CURIOSITY ABOUT EXPERT SYSTEMS

To make managers aware of expert systems, expert system developers can be creative in their "marketing approach" to management. At 3M Corporation, McCullough, who wanted to promote expert systems throughout management, used the Post-It stick-on notes as part of his approach. He had specially printed the phrase "3M Artificial Intelligence: Harvesting Tomorrow's Technology" on these notes and distributed pads of them throughout the company. Since these stick-on notes were used frequently, managers would often see this phrase, provoking their awareness of artificial intelligence/expert systems. McCullough feels that there are four major points when building this foundation of awareness [2]:

- Speak in the jargon of the person to whom you are talking. If the person whose support you are seeking wants to speak in terms of profit and loss or quality control, use those words.
- Strive to communicate, not to impress.
- Don't waste time. If you come up against a brick wall, don't try to run through it.
- Don't force a response or ask for closure. It's important to know that at this point you are planting seeds, not harvesting. Your only goals, at this point, are to raise awareness and create excitement.

Another creative technique for building a foundation of awareness for expert systems is to bring in a speaker to lecture to the company on expert systems or to plan a half-day seminar on expert system technology and applications. By making these opportunities available to management, they might have more incentive to learn about expert systems.

"Hooking" is another way to obtain management's support of expert systems. It is helpful to use when building the expert system prototype to show to management in order to win their support. "Hooking" means adding capabilities to your system that management and/or your potential users would like to have but are unable to obtain easily by any other means [2]. By including two additional production and scheduling reports in a 3M expert system, management was "hooked" on the expert system because now each day these reports could be automatically—instead of manually—produced. These two additional reports hooked both the production and scheduling departments and because of these two reports, the system is used everyday [2].

CASE STUDY: Strategies for Introducing Expert Systems in a Computer Manufacturing Firm

Artificial intelligence (AI), and specifically expert systems, may be a very important and strategic technology to some companies, but oftentimes management isn't aware that AI/expert systems exist. The question then arises: How can one provoke management's awareness of expert systems technology? The answer is: Use a spectrum of approaches to accomplish this goal.

At a company involved in computer configuration management, a combination of approaches was used to instill in management an awareness of expert systems. First, a feasibility study for using expert systems technology in the company's configuration management domain was conducted. The study examined the following areas: Is there a need to develop an aid for facilitating the configuration management function? Can expert systems technology solve that configuration need? How have expert systems been used elsewhere in configuration management? Can expert systems technology be used here at the company? What proof-of-concept expert system prototype can be proposed in the configuration management domain? To find out what the needs were for building an expert configuration system (configurator), both bottom-up and top-down approaches were used. The needs and requirements for a configurator were obtained through interviewing the potential users of the proposed configurator and moving upwards to management (i.e., bottom-up) and the requirements were also derived from interviewing the vice presidents in the company and working top-down through middle management. By using these two approaches, word spread quickly through the company about expert systems technology and the possible idea of building a configurator using expert systems to meet some of the company's needs. Once the feasibility study was completed, it was sent to each vice president in the company for their review.

About a week after the report was received, a memo was circulated to each vice president informing them that an executive briefing would be conducted for about an hour, giving an introduction to artificial intelligence/expert systems and summarizing the findings in the feasibility study. This briefing would be a way of educating, or at the very least, creating an awareness of expert systems technology and how it can be used to help the company. Even though many of the vice presidents could not attend, they sent representatives to the briefing to find out about the findings and learn about expert systems.

However, in order for expert systems technology to be successful within the company, top management's support (at the vice president's level) was needed to sponsor the project. Since the proposed expert system could dramatically affect how the company does its business (hopefully making the process easier and more effective), the backing of top management was needed to "buy off" on this project and incorporate it into the company's strategic plans. So as not to be discouraged, two other strategies were used to provoke an awareness of expert systems and get top management to back the proposed expert system project. The first strategy, borrowed from 3M, was to send a Post-It pad to the president and vice presidents, with each page embossed with the saying "Artificial Intelligence (Expert Systems) is for Real." Following this, the second strategy was to be included on the agenda of the monthly top management staff meeting in order to have a briefing on expert systems and the results of our findings presented.

APPROACH 3: MAKE MANAGEMENT AWARE OF ITS COMPETITION

One way to create an awareness of expert systems is to point out what your competitors are doing. Management's interest would be provoked if you tell them that the competition is using expert systems technology to increase their productivity and revenues. Also, if management wants the company to be state-of-the-art, with a high public image, a good way to achieve this might be to get involved with expert systems.

APPROACH 4: GET THE MANAGERS INVOLVED IN THE EXPERT SYSTEMS DEVELOPMENT PROCESS

One way to create an awareness of expert systems among managers is to get them actively involved in an expert system development effort. Du Pont used a successful "participative" and "supportive" approach for their expert systems development [3]. Mahler, who is in charge of knowledge-based system development at Du Pont, felt that the majority of the organization of the expert system development effort would have to be done by the operating managers (the experts/users). This was done both for corporate culture reasons and because it was necessary in order to give the experts/users a proprietary interest in the system, thereby helping them to understand the benefits and payoffs of the systems [3]. The manager's role was perceived to be one of users, knowledge engineer, system developer, and initiator. In most instances, this multifaceted role helped ensure the manager's involvement in the development of, and interest in, using the final system [3].

Even though managers should be aware of AI/expert systems technology, they need to assess whether AI technology could contribute to the strategic goals of the organization. Eliot mentions some precautionary lessons learned from studying AI cases [7]:

- Determine that AI technology makes sense in your firm on its own merits.

- AI is a changing technology. Just because you started on Lisp machines doesn't mean that PC-based systems aren't useful and can't be integrated into your environment.

- Examine your current technological infrastructure and corporate culture, and pick an AI strategy that matches. If yours is a mainframe-oriented firm, for example, a workstation-based deployment strategy might not make sense.

- The benefits of expert systems are more than just bits of software. Expanding on that thought, for instance, articulating knowledge can improve corporate morale (consider an expert system that evaluates employees for merit raises).

- AI is not magic. It's simply an extension of current programming techniques.

- An AI system that produces economic benefit, but does not achieve its goals, may not be a failure.

- Have a portfolio of AI strategies. From the hardware side, this might mean PC, workstation, and maybe main frame; on the software side, this might mean rules, frames (objects), and different control strategies.

- Don't be afraid to work with vendors or users in allied or even competitive industries.
- AI technologies create new dependencies that could boomerang. Consider the expert system that falls into a competitor's hands, the expert system vendor who goes out of business, or the knowledge engineer who quits.
- To believe that AI is the sole method for solving problems is to be possessed by the technology, and leads to failures.

CONCLUSIONS

There are different ways, as discussed, of provoking managers' awareness of expert systems. Multiple approaches may be used concurrently to make managers aware of or sensitive to expert systems. At a later stage, besides building an in-house capability, as 3M did, for developing expert systems, other implementation strategies can be used by executives for introducing expert systems into the organization. A company might become strategically affiliated with a university or company specializing in expert systems/AI. For example, DEC has close ties with Carnegie-Mellon University. Another strategy is to merge, acquire, or become a major stockholder in a company specializing in expert systems. General Motors, for example, had an interest in Teknowledge, Inc., an expert systems firm. Another major strategy for introducing expert systems into the organization is to expand technology transfer by training people in different groups/divisions throughout the company on expert systems technology. This would create a "distributed environment," as opposed to one centralized, in-house expert systems/AI group, by dispersing expert systems technology throughout different parts of the company. A last strategy is to hire consultants/contractors to help the company get started in expert systems [4].

Whatever approach is used, certainly the first step is building a foundation of awareness of expert systems. After forming this foundation, the next step is to further identify opportunities within the firm where expert systems can contribute to the firm's strategic goals. These opportunities will be discussed in the next two chapters.

REFERENCES

[1]   Leonard-Barton, D., "The Case for Integrative Innovation: An Expert System at Digital," *Sloan Management Review*, MIT, Cambridge, MA, Fall 1987.

[2]   McCullough, T., "Six Steps to Selling AI," *AI Expert*, Miller Freeman Publications, San Francisco, CA, December 1987.

[3]   Dologite, D.G. and R.J. Mockler, "Developing Effective Knowledge-Based Systems: Overcoming Organizational and Individual Behavioral Barriers," *Information Resources Management Journal*, Information Resources Management Association, Middletown, PA, Winter 1989.

[4]   Liebowitz, J., "Approaches for Learning About Expert Systems—A Management Introduction," *Management Decision*, MCB University Press, Bradford, England, Vol. 26, No.5, 1988.

[5]   Beckman, T., "An Expert System in Taxation: The Taxpayer Service Assistant", in *Expert Systems for Business and Management*, J. Liebowitz (ed.), Prentice Hall, Englewood Cliffs, NJ, 1990.

[6]   Gorney, D., "Expert Systems in Health Insurance: Case Studies at Blue Cross of Western Pennsylvania", in *Expert Systems for Business and Management*, J. Liebowitz (ed.), Prentice Hall, Englewood Cliffs, NJ, 1990.

[7]   Eliot, L.B., "Case Studies in AI", Proceedings of Software Development '89 Conference, Miller Freeman Publications, San Francisco, CA, February 1989.

[8]   Interview with Harry C. Reinstein, *SIG-AI Newsletter*, Data Processing Management Association, Worcester, MA, Vol. 1, No. 3, May 1989.

CHAPTER 3

IDENTIFYING OPPORTUNITIES FOR ENHANCING CURRENT OPERATIONS WITHIN THE ORGANIZATION

Once you have instilled in managers an awareness of expert systems, then you need to explore opportunities where expert systems can enhance current operations within the organization in order to improve productivity, performance, and resource utilization. Stand-alone expert systems are becoming less common nowadays, replaced instead with embedded expert systems. Embedded expert systems refer to coupling expert system technology with conventional data processing systems, like management information systems (MIS) and database management systems (DBMS), already existing in the organization. The thrust here is to use expert systems to enhance and improve existing operations within the firm. This chapter will explore various opportunities for integrating expert systems with conventional data processing systems in order to improve current operations.

COUPLING EXPERT SYSTEMS
WITH MANAGEMENT INFORMATION SYSTEMS

A management information systems (MIS) is an automated way of organizing past, present, and projected information on an organization's internal and external intelligence in order to more effectively and efficiently support middle management's decision making. In order to build and maintain an MIS, it requires many resources, both in capital, time, and personpower. Expert systems could facilitate in the development and maintenance of the MIS in various areas.

With MIS programming becoming increasingly complex, expert systems may help automate the planning, design, code generation, and maintenance of the MIS. Some CASE (computer-aided software engineering) tools, like the toolset from KnowledgeWare, incorporate expert system technology; the repository of CASE tools could be a knowledge base in which information about the enterprise and its system is steadily accumulated [1].

Another use for expert systems in the MIS environment is to better inform MIS users on the scope and range of MIS services [1]. MIS users could present problems to the expert system, and the expert system could advise how the user could solve the problem using the organization's MIS capabilities [1].

A third use for expert systems is in helping to manage a large corporate MIS effectively. Expert systems, like IBM's YES, could be designed to assist in the management of the operation of the computer system [1]. Other expert systems could help in other MIS management tasks, like system configuration management, equipment layout planning, and system utilization planning [1].

Other uses for employing expert systems in an MIS environment include [1]:

- Maintenance of large MIS complexes: Individual MIS subsystems could have their own expert maintenance systems to look for potential problems, identify causes of present problems, and suggest remedies for system failures.
- Assistance in performing mainline MIS tasks: In fiscal management tasks, for example, an expert system could assist bookkeepers in assigning a particular invoice to a particular account to ensure that invoices are properly classified.

- Support of the requirements of the strategic, top-level management staff of an organization: In the future, expert systems will incorporate the organization's business model in the knowledge base and will have connectivity to the organization's MIS and executive information systems (EIS).

As illustrated, expert systems offer many opportunities for enhancing a firm's MIS. Many of these expert systems could be embedded within the MIS [11], and certainly some of these expert systems could act in an advisory capacity. The next section looks at coupling expert systems with database management systems.

The following are insights on Expert System Implementation from Dibble and Bostrom [12]:

> The expert system literature has, in general, not addressed the critical issue of implementation. The implicit assumptions appear to be that the expert will be willing, the users receptive, and the organization easily molded. It is obvious from our experience in implementing other types of information systems (IS) that these assumptions are totally unfounded. IS researchers and practitioners have come to view implementation primarily as a process of organizational change and learning. Expert system implementation is no exception. In fact, expert systems may be more difficult to implement because they change control over knowledge and skill, which in turn alters roles responsibilities and power.
>
> If one accepts the notion that expert system implementation is an organizational change process, then the management question becomes: How does one foster 'good' change and achieve successful implementation? Previous IS research has a great deal to say on this issue. Major recommendations from this literature are as follows: (1) view implementation as starting at the beginning of the development process, and (2) understand that implementation success is greatly influenced by the development methodology used. The processes of task selection, expert selection, interface design, end-user involvement, etc. will, therefore, greatly impact implementation success. As a way of bringing about 'good' change, many IS researchers and practitioners are recommending the use of a Socio-Technical Systems (STS) perspective for IS implementations. The STS perspective focuses on integrating technical change (e.g., new information system) into

the organization context recognizing that IS design cannot be isolated from organizational design. The applicability of STS-type development methodologies to expert systems implementation is a researchable issue.

COUPLING EXPERT SYSTEMS
WITH DATABASE MANAGEMENT SYSTEMS

The coupling of expert systems with database management systems is synergistic. Expert systems could be more useful and powerful if they were integrated with existing organizational databases and database management systems (DBMS). In a similar fashion, database management systems could be designed, managed, and maintained better with the application of expert systems technology. Intelligent databases have been a common goal in both the AI and database communities. By marrying AI and database technology, this goal can be achieved.

Harris [2] points out that the coupling of AI and database technology yields intelligent databases in two specific ways. In the first way, rules could be attached to the database record to result in active or intelligent objects. When combined with an inferencing capability, this approach produces a mechanism for adding intelligence to database objects in an understandable and incremental form. In the second way, conceptual definitions can be included that allow the logical view to approximate the conceptual view more accurately [2]. Conceptual definitions are available in high-end natural language interfaces, which are linked to production database systems [2].

Expert system technology can benefit DBMS technology in many other ways. Expert systems can be developed to assist with logical and physical data designs. An expert logical data design system could monitor the human data designer's work and advise the designer of data element omissions in the design and incorrect design specifications [1]. An expert physical data designer system could be developed to assist the DBMS with the task of developing a physical data design from the logical design provided to the DBMS [1]. Another useful application of expert system technology applied to DBMSs is to help incorporate user views into the database. The process of generating new user views of the data might be facilitated by an expert system that uses knowledge about the data model and existing views that have already been developed in order to minimize the number of redundant or overlapping views [3]. Such a tool would be of particular benefit in reaching design decisions when views required for a new application partially match existing ones. Expert systems may also be helpful in the process of developing entity/relationship diagrams.

Kerschberg [4] believes that the system-resident expertise in expert database systems can improve performance by providing intelligent answers. FRED [5], developed by GTE Labs, is an intelligent database front-end which combines database expertise with an intelligent user interface, giving the user substantial help in formulating queries, selecting databases, and interpreting data.

So far, we have only talked about how expert systems can improve DBMSs, but the converse of this is also true: Namely, database technology can improve expert systems. First, the linkage of databases to expert systems allows expert systems to be used for "real-world" applications. Keyes [6] believes that access to these databases is critical for expert systems development. She says that, "There's a billion dollars' worth of corporate data sitting on some mainframe but there's no good explanation of how to connect a highly touted and occasionally expensive expert system tool to this data gold mine [6]." Second, the expert system community can learn from the database community in dealing with subjects such as verification, validation, evaluation, and maintenance. Since the expert systems field is still fairly young, there are numerous areas where the expert systems community can learn from the many years of valuable experience gained by the database community. Last, the database model would contribute to the development of an expert system's knowledge base. A user assistant expert system could be developed which would contain user models and a database model [1]. The user model knowledge would assist the expert system in retrieving the kind of information the user would be interested in getting from the database. The database model would assist the expert system in the development of efficient interactions with the database and the DBMS [1]. Together the database model and user model knowledge would be instrumental in allowing an expert system to provide advice to database users in various phases of database use.

The following are comments from Jerald Feinstein, ICF/Phase

Linear Systems, on the development, database coupling, and transitioning of an expert system built for the Santa Fe Railroad:*

> Our most mature expert system application is the Tracks system that we developed for the Santa Fe Railroad. The purpose of the Tracks system basically is for fleet management—that is, getting the right kinds of cars to the right kinds of customers in the right time. Basically, what we want to do is to satisfy Santa Fe's demand for freight cars to move the freight and at the same time, keep the majority, or actually all of the clients, satisfied. One would think that perhaps that one might use an operations research approach, basically linear programming, to solve this kind of problem. Linear programming was tried by the Santa Fe Railroad first but it was found that the problem itself was much too complicated and computer intensive to be solved by linear programming technology. Since the Santa Fe Railroad had fleet managers and these fleet managers were considered to be incredibly competent by the Railroad, the decision was made to see if the expertise of these fleet managers could be extracted and put in a box—that is, build an expert system. Thus, the expert system called Tracks that we built for the Santa Fe Railroad was actually an expert system designed to emulate the expert fleet managers that the Santa Fe Railroad had. In this case, we were incredibly fortunate because in many of the applications that we get involved in, we are asked to build expert systems where, in fact, the company has no experts and in point of fact they actually have no idea how to solve the problem at hand. The Santa Fe Railroad, however, had a very clear picture of what an expert system was or is and how this system could be used to increase their return on investment. Since the Santa Fe Railroad, in their drive to be a high technology rail provider, really understood expert systems, they were able to find the experts that they wanted to clone and provide easy access to them. Thus, the objective of the Santa Fe Railroad was to "can" the expertise used by their fleet managers and, at the same time, learn exactly how these fleet managers were allocating freight cars in order to meet the demands of the Santa Fe Railroad's clients. Later on, the Railroad felt that they could go into the system, look at the rules that were being used by the experts and see if these rules could somehow be improved in the future. However, Santa Fe was very clear in their initial objective. The objective was only

*Printed with permission from Jerald Feinstein.

to extract the knowledge from their current experts and develop a prototype system that utilized that knowledge. Some of the motivation for this effort came about through the deregulation of the railroad industry. What the Santa Fe Railroad and other railroads really want to do is to minimize the size of their fleet while still meeting 100% of their customer demands for freight cars. The audience in this case would, of course, be the Santa Fe Fleet Management Office. In this case the fleet managers themselves would be the first users of the system; after that, the system then could be migrated down to people who perhaps were not necessarily an expert in fleet management, but smart enough to use the system; and in a sense the system would, it was felt by the Santa Fe Railroad, be almost like a training device. These neophyte experts or trainees would be able to work with the system to become better fleet managers ultimately. The application itself, as I mentioned, was fleet management. That is getting the right kind of car to the right kind of person, the right kind of client in the proper time. The same time to determine from what location certain cars are drawn and where those cars go in order to minimize empty time. Ultimately, I think minimizing empty time was the goal of the Santa Fe Railroad, however, ultimately what we want to do was to maximize profit which doesn't necessarily relate to minimizing empty car miles. Thus, what a fleet manager is really doing is functioning in a way similar to an expert pool or billiards player. He's not necessarily interested in the initial allocation of cars but he or she is also very much interested in where those cars are going to end up. So what we're really looking at is an end-stage planning exercise where expertise is used. Now these expert fleet managers have access to all of the Santa Fe's computerized databases. Now what these databases are, essentially, are cars by type, where they are, the condition of the cars, etc. Then the fleet manager decides from where to take these cars, link them up with trains and allocate them to the clients. Now what this means is that the cars are often transported from one location to a client's site or a customer's site. And the customer site is usually a siding, therefore, these cars are delivered to the customer's railroad siding to sit there for some period of time, sometimes perhaps maybe a day, two days, a week, maybe two weeks to be loaded and after they are loaded the cars are transported to their final destinations. The expert fleet manager also has access to various perhaps small models, simulations, small linear programming, and tools that allow that person to make quick trial solutions. Therefore, what we have to do with the expert system itself, since we were emulating a real-world flesh and blood expert was to enable the expert system itself to tie into the numerous databases, actually mainframe databases, that the Santa Fe Railroad had the same time the expert system had to be tied into the various models and small linear programming routines that the expert himself had access to. In this way we were able to create an expert system that not only emulated an expert, but also actually interacted with the Santa Fe databases and models in the same way that the real world expert did. The development cycle followed the normal development cycle of an expert system, in fact, it was a textbook case. Again, since the Santa Fe Railroad really understood what expert systems technology was all about we didn't have to go through an education phase in trying to educate the client as to what expert systems were, how they could increase the return on investment and thus, phase 1 was essentially familiarizing ourselves with fleet management and how the fleet managers went about allocating freight cars. The other part of the effort was to familiarize ourselves with the computer files, databases, and models that these fleet managers actually interacted with or used when making an allocation. So in our sense, we have to familiarize ourselves with not only what knowledge that the fleet managers used (actually exercise their expertise of allocating freight cars) but more so every aspect of how the Santa Fe Railroad went about their business in terms of evaluating how well the fleet managers did their job and also how all of the databases were actually tied together. This was important because we realized that the final expert system we put together would have to access all the databases in the same way that the real experts did and also to emulate how the experts actually used their day-to-day models in making our forecasts as to how many freight cars might be needed next week, next month or in some other future period.

Next after we extracted some of the knowledge what we did is we started prototyping the system itself. This was done in the usual rapid prototyping or onion-skin mold where we took some of the expertise, packaged it in the expert system shell and took i' and demonstrated it to the Santa Fe executives to show them essentially what the expert system was and how it actually allocated freight cars using the limited knowledge that we had already captured. To digress a bit, what we did too, is we were working not only with Santa Fe's Research and Development Department, we were also working very closely with the user group. In fact, the user group was viewed as the ultimate client and thus, we became incredibly familiar with all aspects of fleet management and what the users actually were doing in their day-to-day operations. Now this included actually going out on trains, observing the freight yards, the signalling and basically all aspects of the Santa Fe Railroad's business as it related to fleet management. Thus, as the system evolved from nothing to the first viewings of the prototype there were never any surprises because we were working very closely with the fleet management people as well as the Research and Development Department so that all people actually participated in system development. Currently, the system passed its prototype configuration and we're in the midst of migrating the expert system to the mainframe in an IBM environment. At this point, it becomes incredibly important in migrating into the mainframe environment, this is the part of expert systems development that most people don't talk about, and that's this: When people think about developing expert systems, they think about artificial intelligence, knowledge engineering, knowledge acquisition and some of the more exotic areas of artificial intelligence. But when we build a prototype, go beyond the prototype stage, then we have to take that expert system and actually embed it into the infrastructure of the client, which in this case happens to be an IBM mainframe environment. Things become a little less interesting for I would say, the younger types of individuals who were schooled in artificial intelligence applications. The reason I say this is this, because in some cases more than half of a real expert system application, I'm not talking about little prototypes but things that a large company is really going to be using, has to be integrated with all their operations in a mainframe environment and when you start doing this, you start tying things into a database, starting to work with database query languages, start to work with many of the kinds of things that people who work in the AI area don't seem to be interested in the detail work of making an application really function. For this area we are using another kind of individual, not the classic AI person, but the traditional kind of software person who understands databases, understands software architecture and knows how to embed any kind of software system within a larger one, because even though we're working in what we call an expert systems environment, when we look at the chip level it's all bits, zeros and ones. The point I'm trying to make is that, I guess, in any real world application, the traditional AI or expert systems portion of it may be only half of the job, the other half of the job is embedding that expert system into the what shall I call it, the conventional computer infrastructure of a large corporation, and that is making it work in harmony with all of their other databases and all of their other computer models the same way that a real expert might.

Since right now we're still, I guess, implementing the system in the mainframe environment, I can't really comment on the usage of the system and what payoffs that it has, except that when the system was first proposed one of the things that we did, one of the things that we always do in this kind of application, we put together a very conservative return on investment analysis for the client to show how expert systems technology can really payoff in terms of such fundamental financial figures, using certain fundamental financial tools such as return on investment analysis, because we can show that by using this technology one can increase the return on investment, it just makes sense to go ahead and do it (Not only increase the return on investment but say increase it beyond what you can do using other options). Remembering, of course, that the cost of doing nothing is often not zero.

In how we're getting the expert system to be accepted by the users within the client organization, I think, is simple in this case because the users themselves were very sophisticated in the sense that they really understood expert systems technology. The Santa Fe Railroad people were not your average client; they understood technology and they understood what technology could do for them. What we did was help them implement what they wanted to do and that was to build an expert system to emulate their fleet managers. Since we were working with the users every day and developed a good rapport with the users in working on site, we had little difficulty in getting the system accepted in a sense that as long as the system worked and did essentially the same as what the current fleet managers did we would be in good shape and the expert system ultimately would be used.

On describing the user training strategies, these were evolutionary in that by actually building the system partially on site and working with the Santa Fe Railroad people to implement the system, we had a rather unique opportunity in that the users were not just introduced to the system, they would be fairly familiar with the system by the time it was implemented. The users themselves were instrumental in building the system so that it wasn't I guess the situation where a system was dropped on someone's lap and they were asked to use something that they actually didn't partake in developing.

In the documentation guidelines for the system itself, a large organization has requirements for documentation of software systems. What we're doing is right now we've agreed to document the expert system along the lines of Santa Fe documentation standards. However, in the future what we'll probably do is help the Santa Fe Railroad modify the documentation standards to incorporate special standards for expert systems use. For example, expert systems specifications and expert systems evolution are usually done through rapid prototyping and were evolutionary rather than developing complex standards and specifications where code is only written late in the project. So what we're tying to do is help the Santa Fe Railroad to modify the software documentation standards to incorporate the new technology of expert systems.

On the topic of user support services, what we plan to have are things like help desks and meetings among the users. We haven't decided yet with the users what would be an optimum frequency for meetings. We envision that in the beginning we'd like to have perhaps daily meetings going off perhaps to weekly meetings then perhaps monthly meetings, but we're not sure as to the break points as to when the daily meetings might turn into weekly meetings. Some other user support services, of course, would be a help desk. In the beginning, what we would be doing would be providing the Santa Fe with user support in a sense that if somebody had a question on how some aspect of the system worked we would have somebody available to help them.

Maintenance strategies—by maintenance what I mean is upgrade. What we would probably do along with the help desk as a result of the daily, weekly and then monthly meetings, would be to identify specific items for change—that is, how to make the system more usable, what additional rules perhaps did we miss, and ways to get those new rules integrated into the system. In addition to rules that we might have missed, one of the benefits of expert systems is that it allows you to kind of peruse the knowledge base to see how you really went about doing things. What this allows us to do is to not only peruse the knowledge base but actually make it better. We'll have the luxury perhaps of changing certain rules in very subtle ways, kind of experimenting or actually letting the fleet managers experiment in the way they've been doing things to see if they can fine tune their system and actually develop better rules. These rules that would be say rules that we either missed or rules that would come about later on to make the system better would be reviewed perhaps at these weekly or monthly meetings and at some point could be implemented or would be implemented into the rule base for the system itself.

Now in regards to legal distribution issues, one of the nice things about an expert system is that the rules or the allocation rules in this case, for fleet management are available for someone to look at in plain English. It's not something like computer code that one might have to be some sort of computer expert to figure out what was really happening. Secondly, fleet management is not something that could cause a problem where a railroad or an organization would face a liability issue. For example, if we got into such areas as railroad signalling, control, actually modifying a rolling stock, there could be issues of liability, but in this case what we're doing is taking an expert's knowledge or something that resembles plain English rules, letting the expert review those rules and then very slowly in a very structured way testing the application of those rules to real world situations, to getting freight cars to a customer's location. Something that both the Santa Fe Railroad and our legal staff agree that there would probably be no liability issues involved. And on that basis we've been going ahead on this.

As far as distribution issues go, this is not a system that is going to be distributed to a lot of elements within the Santa Fe Railroad. It's a system that will reside in a mainframe environment and that disks are not going to be floating around, and only the people involved in fleet management will have access to that system. So that any updates of the system will be strictly controlled and there will never be any old versions of the system floating around for inadvertent use. So again it's nice having a mainframe environment in a sense that we don't have a problem of many different versions floating around the user community in that they might have a chance of using an outdated system.

The guidelines that I might have or advice for transitioning of expert systems or expert systems shells into an organization is this: I, myself, am a fan of the Du Pont or Weyerhauser model where expert system technology is injected into the organization at the grass roots level. This is the same model that the Santa Fe Railroad has used—money, resources have been expended so that people throughout the company can go out and take seminars, buy expert systems software and dabble in the technology. The reason why this is a good idea is because the people who have the requirements themselves are the ones who best know how to implement expert systems technology within their own corporation. That is they know the technology, they know their job, they know how the corporation works; they're the ones who will know how to implement this technology best. And what they can do is when you go out initially and take a seminar or so in building expert systems and knowledge acquisition and knowledge engineering, you also may have a consultant or company come into work with your people side by side in building your first application so that the technology is really injected into your own corporation. If you're working side by side with experts and absorbing the new technology so that ultimately the technology becomes commonplace within your organization, you feel comfortable with it; it's not viewed as some sort of new black magic and you can get a good return on investment in this. What we're talking about is this: If we're not talking about a Lisp application or the fact that we might be using some expert system shell, we're talking about taking expertise and putting into a computer and using it to get a good return on investment. Many companies are learning today that what they really have to sell is expertise because many companies have found out too that a lot of their people have, I guess, come on board right after World War II and those people are retiring on mass and these companies have found out that after these people go they really have nothing to sell. I'm talking about chemical companies that are making new products, rubber companies, plastic companies, consulting companies and what have you. Those companies are finding out that what they really sell is expertise and the expertise of their employees.

Now when we go back and I mentioned earlier that an expert system is nothing more than a computer program, the question often comes up as to why do you have to use a shell, why not write the expert system in FORTRAN, PL/1 or some other language? And what I say is this: When you build a database application we use something like dBase, Oracle, we don't usually use assembly language or necessarily Cobol to build a system from scratch unless the system requirements are so different that none of these shells or development environments actually can do a better job. So what we're saying is the only reason that we're using shells right now is because shells allow us to build our systems quicker, better and more cheaply than building them from scratch and this is a very important concept to understand because in our seminars that we give, this is something that comes up all the time. They'll say well I can do this in FORTRAN or I can do this in BASIC or I can do this in Cobol and our answer to this all the time is that if you can build any of these systems better and less expensively using any other method, then do so. Because the only thing that an expert system really is again is computer software that emulates an expert.

The last point that I'd like to make concerns the importance of institutionalizing an expert system after it's developed. And I'd like to say this is because of an interesting example. This example was an expert system that was built for a client that exceeded its specifications. The system, I think and the client thought, was a basic good system that did exactly what it was intended to do. The problem was that the developer, our client, was not the ultimate client organization. This system was basically dropped into the lap of a client who had, say, only limited involvement with expert system development. Not only that, our client had decided that since it was a captive organization, that they didn't want to fund institutionalization of the expert system, that they were just going to drop the expert system in their lap and require them to use it. Well, that's not exactly the case, they were going to fund training but that was about it, no help, etc. Well, what happened was that the expert system was never used, the reasoning behind that was obscure, it was something that for one reason or another, there was a lot of foot dragging, there were objections to using the system for one reason or another, but the real objection came from the fact that it wasn't (1) invented in the client organization and (2) something that we knew. Something the client now knows is that unless you institutionalize or set up help desks, set up meetings with the user groups to further develop the system, and have the user group itself develop what we call system ownership or some sort of identifying with the system itself, the system is doomed for failure. And this is something that not only we've experienced, but in talking to other systems developers, we've seen it happen again and again. So my point is that when you develop an expert system, make sure that the ultimate users are involved and develop things like we call institutionalization strategies, get the user management on board, get the ultimate users themselves on board, develop a strategy for weekly or monthly meetings to help upgrade the system and make the system more useful for the users because if you don't do this the system isn't going to work.

Besides the synergistic effects between expert systems and DBMSs, expert systems can improve existing decision support system (DSS) technology. A DSS is an automated tool that supports the tasks and activities associated with strategic planning and decision making. Expert systems can be linked with DSSs. One useful application of this is to use an expert system to explain some of the changes in values in a spreadsheet. For example, a spreadsheet might indicate that sales increased by 10 percent from one year to the next. But an expert system can enhance the explanation process by explaining that, for example, sales increased by 10 percent because international sales increased due to greater market penetration into foreign universities, while expenses remained roughly the same as those in the previous year. Expert systems have already been developed that tie into spreadsheets and DBMS packages. One system calculates whether travel funds are available for use and why one may not be able to obtain funding for another trip (a message might state that one has spent $600 in travel funds thus far out of $600 allocated and that because one has consumed one's budget, additional requests for traveling must be authorized by the regional manager) [7].

Combinations of DSSs and expert systems might be used to replace operations research models with multiple rules, or heuristics. For example, PATRIARCH, a DSS-expert system under development at Carnegie-Mellon University, combines operations research models with scheduling heuristics to make manufacturing decisions. Using DSSs for manufacturing planning decisions and expert systems for approximating solutions in scheduling steps in manufacturing would be a worthwhile vehicle.

WORDS OF CAUTION IN INTEGRATING EXPERT SYSTEMS WITH CONVENTIONAL DATA PROCESSING SYSTEMS

In selecting applications for expert systems, the KISS rule applies: Keep It Simple but Significant [8]. Choose applications for expert systems that [8]:

- Are real. Don't try to solve problems that don't exist—you'll only create systems nobody will use.
- Fit in with your organization's future directions and plans.
- Are of manageable size.
- Are doable. Don't tackle an undefined problem or a problem nobody knows how to solve.
- Have sources of knowledge and experts willing to cooperate.
- Have measurable benefits.

In thinking about integrating expert systems with existing data processing systems, remember to consider database and network capabilities. The database question hinges on, "Do users absolutely require immediate read/write access to corporate data, or can they survive with downloaded data [6]?" Network capabilities should be carefully considered in terms of what needs to be connected and how difficult is it to access data via your network. The ultimate system for delivery to the user should be easy to use, with the seams transparent [6].

CONCLUSIONS

In the mid-1990s, databases and rule-based systems will be fully integrated, embedded, and compatible with standard software, hardware, and operating systems [9,10]. Merging rule-based programming with database applications will allow organizations to incorporate business goals and rules directly into their information systems [9]. As presented here, there are certainly many opportunities for integrating expert systems with traditional data processing systems in order to improve operations.

REFERENCES

[1] Martin, J. and S. Oxman, *Building Expert Systems: A Tutorial*, Prentice Hall, Englewood Cliffs, NJ, 1988.

[2] Harris, L.R., "The Marriage of AI and Database Technology," *AI Expert*, Miller Freeman Publications, San Francisco, CA, March 1987.

[3] American Management Systems, Inc., "Final Report: Knowledge Base System Support Study for the U.S. Army Information Systems Command-Pentagon," Arlington, VA, August 21, 1985.

[4] Kerschberg, L., "Guest Editor's Introduction: Expert Database Systems," *IEEE Expert*, IEEE, Los Alamitos, CA, Winter 1988.

[5] Jakobson, G., C. Lafond, E. Nyberg, and G. Piatetsky-Shapiro, "An Intelligent Database Assistant," *IEEE Expert*, IEEE, Los Alamitos, CA, Summer 1986.

[6] Keyes, J., "Expert Systems and Corporate Databases," *AI Expert*, Miller Freeman Publications, San Francisco, CA, May 1989.

[7] Liebowitz, J., *The Dynamics of Decision Support Systems and Expert Systems*, Dryden Press, Hinsdale, Illinois, 1990.

[8] Smith, D., "Implementing Real World Expert Systems," *AI Expert*, Miller Freeman Publications, San Francisco, CA, December 1988.

[9] Cohen, B., "Merging Expert Systems and Databases," *AI Expert*, Miller Freeman Publications, San Francisco, CA, February 1989.

[10] Risch, T., R. Reboh, P. Hart, and R. Duda, "A Functional Approach to Integrating Database and Expert Systems," *Communications of the ACM*, Association for Computing Machiner, New York, Vol. 31, No. 12, December 1988.

[11] Gallagher, J.P., *Knowledge Systems for Business: Integrating Expert Systems & MIS*, Prentice Hall, Englewood Cliffs, NJ, 1988.

[12] Dibble, D. and R.P. Bostrom, "Managing Expert Systems Projects: Factors Critical for Successful Implementation," Proceedings of the 1987 ACM SIGBDP-SIGCPR Conference, New York: Association for Computing Machinery, 1987.

CHAPTER 4

IDENTIFYING OPPORTUNITIES FOR NEW APPLICATIONS WITHIN THE ORGANIZATION

In Chapter 3, we identified opportunities for using expert systems to enhance traditional data processing systems in the organization. Now we will take a look at coupling expert systems with leading edge technology in order to create new opportunities for applications within the organization. We will specifically describe the merging of expert systems with hypertext for intelligent text management.

EXPERTEXT

"Expertext" has been coined [1] as a term that denotes the merging of expert systems with hypertext. Hypertext, at its most basic level, is a DBMS that lets you connect screens of information using associative links [2]. Imagine this scenario [3]:

. . . sitting at your computer and bringing up a hypertext system on music. You begin to read about Mozart. When you wonder about Austrian history, you simply highlight the text and request more information with a mouse click or a few keystrokes. To find images of old Salzburg, you use the same process. And to hear the piano concerto? The same.

Like a relational database management system for text, hypertext lets developers control large amounts of textual information for easy access by users. So what does it add to expert systems? Hypertext complements the structured logic of expert systems with its associative or browsing approach [4]. Users can proceed through an expert system until they can go no further, then call a hypertext card and begin to browse through other types of information until they find what they need to progress within the initial system [4].

The ideal model is a methodology for providing the user with a way of navigating through a complex knowledge base so that he/she is assured of being exposed to the main points while remaining free to explore tangential ideas of interest [5]. In this model, a layered knowledge approach is used, whereby the top layer is the minimum information, and deeper layers are, in order, expanded key ideas, explanation of key terms, related information impact, and then ancillary information of interest. By using a layered knowledge approach, the user does not feel his/her quest for knowledge being stifled by a lack of opportunity to ask and receive answers to questions that arise in the course of the knowledge transfer [5].

To qualify as hypertext, a system must use a more sophisticated notion of links and must provide more machine support for its links than merely typing file names after a text editor prompt [6]. According to Conklin [6], several systems have some of the attributes of hypertext but do not qualify. These include window systems, file systems, most outline processors, text formatting systems, and database management systems [6].

OPPORTUNITIES FOR EXPERT SYSTEMS AND HYPERTEXT

Let's look at an example where the merging of expert systems and hypertext could be very useful. CESA [7] is an expert system prototype being developed at the Navy Center for Applied Research in

Artificial Intelligence for helping in U.S. Defense research contracting. CESA (COTR Expert System Aid) is aimed at helping the Contracting Officer Technical Representative (COTR) in providing advice on a contract's pre-award phase. Specifically, CESA advises the COTR on such pre-award areas as what forms are needed to make up a procurement request package, synopsis requirements, routing of documents, advice on completing selected pre-award forms, and a host of other topics. Hypertext, although not implemented yet in CESA, could greatly enhance the usability of CESA. CESA now recommends what forms are needed to make up an adequate procurement request package for the specific needs of the COTR. CESA also provides advice on how to complete selected pre-award forms. (Appendix A provides an in-depth case study of CESA.) Hypertext could be tied into CESA to allow the user to then view these pre-award forms, and then click onto areas in the form about which the user has questions. Hypertext would then allow the user to obtain some explanation/description of that particular section within the form, and the user could even get a further elaboration within that section using hypertext links. By merging expert systems with hypertext, the user might greatly benefit from this marriage. Figure 4-1 shows some sample screens from a CESA-hypertext sample session, using KnowledgePro, which was to help the user complete a Justification and Approval form.

Already, there are various examples of expert system and hypertext "marriages." Some of these "married" and "strictly hypertext" tools and applications include [5,8,9]:

- MacSMARTS—tool for permitting the developer to create links between an expert system application and HyperCard.
- Instant-Expert Plus—tool for linking expert systems with HyperCard.
- HyperX—hypertext tutorial on teaching how inference engine mechanisms work.
- Staxpert—relatively fast-executing expert system shell contained entirely in the HyperCard environment.
- Guide—hypertext product.
- Knowledge Navigator—part HyperCard, part object-oriented programming language, part CD-ROM, and part expert system.

DEPARTMENT OF THE NAVY

NAVAL RESEARCH LABORATORY

JUSTIFICATION FORM FOR OTHER THAN FULL
AND OPEN COMPETITION

Press space during program to continue; press
ESC after typing in the text windows
Press F3 to select highlighted words and F4 to
view the word(s) highlighted

Designed by
Daniel Chian
Laura Davis
Jay Liebowitz

F1 Help   F5 Evaluate   F7 Edit   Pg 1 of 1
Space Cont.   F6 Display KB F8 DOS   F10 Quit

KnowledgePro_____
Does the Department of the Navy, contracting
through the Naval Research Laboratory, propose
to enter into a contract on other than a full
and open competitive basis?
Use cursor keys to choose option and enter to
select.

```
    ┌──────────────┐
    │  [1 yes]     │
    │   2 no       │
    └──────────────┘
```

F1 Help   F5 Evaluate   F7 Edit
              F6 Display KB F8 DOS   F10   Quit

Figure 4-1   Sample Hypertext screens for completing a justification and
approval form.

KnowledgePro————————————————————
State the nature and/or description of the
[supplies/services required] to meet the
needs of the Naval Research Laboratory and the
estimated value including all options.
Example for question 3.

┌─Example: Requirements——————————————————┐
│ NRL requires that this hardware be
│ operational to the fullest extent possible
│ and the hardware and software be current
│ with the latest revisions from the
│ manufacturer.   │
└───┘

F1 Help   F5 Evaluate   F7 Edit   Pg 1 of 1
Space Cont.   F6 Display KB F8 DOS   F10 Quit

KnowledgePro————————————————————
State the nature and/or description of the
supplies/services required, to meet the needs
of the Naval Research Laboratory and the
estimated value including all options.
[Example for question 3]

┌─Requirements: press ESC when done——————————┐
│ NRL requires that this hardware be
│ operational to the fullest extent possible
│ and that the hardware and software be
│ current with the latest revisions from the
│ manufacturer. NRL needs a service contract
│ in place to repair broken equipment and to
│ provide the latest hardware and software
│ revisions and upgrades as released by XYZ
│ Corp.   │
└───┘

F1 Help F3 Select F5 Evaluate F7 Edit Page
Esc Exit F4 View   F6 Disp. KB F8 DOS F10 Quit

Figure 4-1   (continued)

KnowledgePro_____
You must have an identification of the
statutory authority permitting other than
full or open competition (See FAR 6.302)
usually 10 U.S.C. 2304(c) (1) and FAR
8.302-1 - Only one responsible source or
Unsolicited Proposal; -or- 10 U.S.C.
2304(c)(2) and FAR 6.302-2 - [Unusual and
Compelling Urgency]

```
_Urgency_____
If urgency is used, describe in paragraph
5 what harm would come to the Government
if the date is missed. Note that failure
to plan and the length of the procurement
process are not justification.
```

F1 Help   F5 Evaluate   F7 Edit   Pg 1 of 1
Space Cont.   F6 Display KB   F8 DOS   F10 Quit

KnowledgePro_____
You must have an identification of the
statutory authority permitting other than
full or open competition (See FAR 6.302)
usually 10 U.S.C. 2304(c)(1) and FAR
6.302-1 - Only one responsible source or
Unsolicited Proposal; -or- 10 U.S.C.
2304(c)(2) and FAR 6.302-2 - Unusual and
Compelling Urgency.

```
[1 10 U.S.C. 2304(c)(1) and FAR 6.302-1]
 2 10 U.S.C. 2304(c)(2) and FAR 6.302-2
 3 other
```

F1 Help   F3 Select F5 Evaluate F7 Edit
          F4 View   F6 Disp. KB F8 DOS   F10 Quit

Figure 4-1 (continued)

- KnowledgePro—an IBM PC based expert system and hypertext product.
- Exsys Professional—an expert system shell that incorporates hypertext capabilities.
- Hyperties—an instructional, interactive encyclopedia system.
- 1st Class-HT—an expert system development software enhanced with hypertext.
- VP Expert—an expert system shell with hypertext capabilities.
- KRS—software system specially designed to access CD-ROM databases consisting of both text and graphic information.
- Business File Vision—Macintosh hypertext product.
- HyperCard—Apple product for combining hypertext and expert systems.
- KMS—a hypertext product.
- Marcon—a DBMS with hypertext-like indexes.
- Thoth II—a system that embeds semantics into hypertext.
- Notes—a hypertext writer's tool.
- DIF—a hypertext system with software engineering tools.
- Xanadu—a worldwide hypertext library.
- NoteCards—an information analyst's support tool.
- Opus I—a hypergraphics and text information program.
- WinDOS—a hypertext DOS reference manual.
- HyperPad—provides hypertext linking through buttons and an object-oriented scripting language.

CASE STUDY: Intelligent Insurance Systems

Jerry Burg, a former insurance executive and now president of Intelligent Insurance Systems of Sherman Oaks, California, is writing an expert system based on KnowledgePro for insurance agents and brokers. As he explains [11]:

> Hypertext is what got me excited about expert systems. Executives need additional information to make decisions, and it's not always easy to know where to get it. This is especially true of insurance company underwriters. Common resources, such as

badly indexed manuals, are a chore to search. Most manuals are written in linear fashion, but people don't look for information that way. They jump in and out, looking for what they need. Who wants to spend two hours looking for one little piece of information? But hypertext provides information on an 'as needed' basis because users can pursue only the information they want. It lets a user get at key concepts any time. That's important from the standpoint of productivity.

HYPERMEDIA

As videodisc technology comes of age, there is growing interest in the extension of hypertext to the more general concept of "hypermedia." With it, the elements which are networked together can be text, graphics, digitized speech, audio recordings, pictures, animation, film clips, and possibly tastes, odors, and tactile sensations [6]. KnowledgeSet Corporation already has the Graphic Knowledge Retrieval System which accesses CD-ROM databases providing both a subject-oriented and full-text search capability [10]. The link between expert systems and hypermedia can be illustrated in the following way. Imagine walking into your neighborhood video club. To help you with your search, you log onto a computer that has an expert system for advising you on what tapes may be appropriate for your interests. If you want more information about a particular tape, you use the hypertext capability to provide descriptions about that movie and you could use hypertext to "dig deeper" to find out who stars in the movie, for example. If it interests you, you then use the interactive CD-ROM link to actually see a 20 second color excerpt from that movie. Finally, you are convinced and you check out that tape, assuming it is available. The availability of the tapes suggests the need for the expert system to link into the perpetual inventory status of the tapes in the store.

This example beautifully illustrates the viability of linking expert systems with hypermedia. This application doesn't exist presently in the video stores, but it certainly will in the near term. Other useful applications of using expert systems with hypergraphics (part of hypermedia) include:

- Creating great visually oriented intelligent information management systems that even a novice can use. For example, a typical application might include apartment management to visually show the location of each unit with buttons to show the tenant's records, maintenance records, or vacancy records. Another application might be theatrical management to show the location of seats and which seats are unsold and which seats are held by season ticket holders [9].

- Developing trouble-shooting systems/diagnostic assistants with the aid of expert systems and hypergraphics.

CONCLUSIONS

As discussed, the use of hypertext and hypermedia, in general, with expert systems can create new opportunities for improving or enhancing the activities of an organization. Managers must look down the road to identify how new technology can help their organization in better meeting their operating and strategic goals. One possibility is to couple expert system technology with hypertext, if the application warrants such an approach. It should be recognized, however, that there are problems with using hypertext. One of the most difficult parts of creating a hypertext system is creating sound underlying data models that can be maintained [2]. A second concern with hypertext systems is that they may be only suited for new application development; converting existing applications to hypertext is a difficult task because the file structures are so different [2]. Over time, some of these problems will be ameliorated, but it is the manager's responsibility to keep abreast of these developments.

REFERENCES

[1]   Rada, R., "Expertext: The Synergy Between Expert Systems and Hypertext," *Expert Systems With Applications: An International Journal*, Pergamon Press, Elmsford, New York, Vol. 1, No. 1, 1990.

[2]   Fiderio, J., "Hypertext: A Grand Vision," *Byte*, McGraw-Hill, Peterborough, NH, October 1988.

[3]   Tazelaar, J.M., "Hypertext: In Depth," *Byte*, McGraw-Hill, Peterborough, NH, October 1988.

[4]   1st Class Expert Systems, Inc., "1st Class-HT Marketing Information," Wayland, MA, 1989.

[5]   Shafer, D., "Hypermedia and Expert Systems: A Marriage Made in Hyper Heaven," *Hyperage*, May-June, 1988.

[6]   Conklin, J., "Hypertext: An Introduction and Survey," *IEEE Computer*, IEEE, New York, September 1987.

[7]   Liebowitz, J., L.C. Davis, and W.F. Harris, "CESA: An Expert System Prototype for U.S. Defense Research Contracting," *Expert Systems for Business and Management*, Prentice Hall, Englewood Cliffs, NJ, 1990.

[8]   Begeman, M.L. and J. Conklin, "Hyper Activity," *Byte*, McGraw-Hill, Peterborough, NH, October 1988.

[9]   Anacker, P., "Thinking Tools: Part IV," *PC AI*, November/December 1988.

[10]   KnowledgeSet Corporation, The Graphic Knowledge Retrieval System Demo Disk, Monterey, CA, 1989.

[11]   Patton, C., "Professionals Adopting Pint-Sized Expert Systems," *Info World*, Menlo Park, CA, October 10, 1988.

PART III

Implementing/Institutionalizing
Expert Systems
in the Organization

CHAPTER 5

USER TRAINING STRATEGIES FOR INSTITUTIONALIZING EXPERT SYSTEMS

After identifying opportunities where expert systems can benefit the firm, the next step involves the actual development of the expert system. Dan DeSalvo, from MCI, and Lashon Booker, from the Naval Research Laboratory, explain, in the following section, the development and implementation of their respective expert system projects. Liebowitz and DeSalvo [1] and Liebowitz [2] thoroughly explain the structured life cycle development of expert systems. (Appendix A discusses these steps in the context of CESA's development.)

The focus of this chapter and the rest of this book is to explain ways for ensuring proper institutionalization of an expert systems after it has already been built and tested. One critical element of this institutionalization process is the need for having proper user training on the use of the expert system. This chapter addresses this need.

THE IMPORTANCE OF USER TRAINING

Bailey [3] states that a system may be well designed and have adequate written instructions, but if users are not taught exactly what they are to do and how best to do it, then the probability of having errors is high. Inadequate user training can be very costly to an organization. The Social Security Administration found this out in the early 1970s when they installed a new computer-based system for their operations. Unfortunately, they later found that the system had sent out somewhere between $400 million and $1 billion in overpayments during the first two years of the new system's operations. The major reason given by Social Security officials for these costly errors was not inadequate software or a faulty computer, but "poorly trained personnel [3]." In the early 1980s, the Internal Revenue Service installed a new computer system to handle tax processing, but problems resulted because, as one reason, the staff was not properly trained on how to operate the system.

A key point to remember is technology transfer. No matter how well an expert system performs, it won't do any good if no one can or will use it [13]. A well-trained knowledge engineer can ease this problem: Involve the people who will use the expert system in the development phase [13]. Ed Feigenbaum, at the Texas Instruments Third AI Symposium, reiterated this point. He feels that one of the failures in expert system projects can occur in the failure to understand adequately the state of mind, to position and explain the state of acceptability of your system to the end user. Feigenbaum explains that if you don't understand what the conditions are under which your expert system will be acceptable to that user, you may have a technical success—but a technology transfer failure.

The following are comments from Dan DeSalvo, MCI Telecommunications Corporation, on the development and implementation of one of MCI's expert systems, PRICER:*

> When you talk about the most mature expert system at MCI—
> that's Pricer—Officially the MCI corporate pricing model. Pricer
> will price the quotation. And the issue here is not that it necessarily should be an expert system—and there are a lot of different
> ways to approach this—but that the expert systems technology

*Printed with permission from Daniel DeSalvo.

would, in this case be KBMS on the IBM mainframe, which gives us the ability to write a much more robust, maintainable application. It allows us easily and in a cross-productive way to do some things that we otherwise probably would avoid doing simply because it would be too much effort. Things like making it really "goofproof." It's very hard to come up with a bad answer—a totally bad answer. It is in a sense an expert system because there were experts involved in its construction. But I sort of take the view that any good system built by people who know what the job that has to be done consists of is an expert system. I mean, you have to have somebody who knows the business function that has to be performed and that person is usually classified as the domain expert.

The target user community is the field marketing group. The marketing rep has a tremendous task because our environment is very fast moving and continually growing and we have some products out there—System One and System Plus, 800, advance services and those sorts of products—that are very hot on the market right now. And they service a broad business level. In other words, you're only going to want to make up individual quotations for the really huge company that's going to have all kinds of different services put in there and they are going to need a custom tailored application. On the other hand what we have here are businesses that really have very respectable services and we are eventually tailoring our services to those customers on a very broad basis and want to be able to keep up with them. Now here we have a situation where we are introducing new products left and right and there are variations on products and new discount schedules because it's a very competitive market. In fact, in those areas of the market, we are the market leaders and it's very difficult to stay ahead introducing products and safety for sales people and train them also in how to use the system. So we are sort of taking the attitude that the system should expedite the sale; in fact it should take less training to use the system than to do it otherwise. And also they shouldn't have to learn how to use the user interface on the system—to go through training for that. That doesn't make sense. So what we developed is an application that is very simple, very easy to use, and gives the sales rep the opportunity to work with the customer and do what sales reps do, which is understand the customer needs and figure out how to tailor our services to their requirements and that sort of thing. The leverage is that our results are phenomenal because what we are really doing is using the technology in line with the business function. Instead of making the task a slave to the way we built the application, we are serving their business function with the application. I will say that it has changed the way we do business at MCI. It has allowed us to do business more the way we like to do business—which is very customer-oriented or service-oriented—and be very aggressive in trying to fit our products and services to the customer. And now we know that we don't need a long turnaround time to train because the systems are very adaptable. If you look at the way we've constructed it we effectively have a module or an expert system for each of our products in the Pricer: You go in, you log on to a very simple sequence, you feed it a handful of very simple numbers, and it comes back with an answer. In the process, it stops you from things that you didn't put in. So basically you don't need to be able to know effectively much more than two things: how to log on to the system and hit enter all the time, and the other is what your customer is doing. And basically, for the products we have, that amounts to some very simple things like new basic usage and some calling pattern stuff which is in most cases available right off the bill.

It's interesting about how we gained acceptance by the users, and there are a couple of stories about that: one is how we got sort of the rapid turn-around on projects and we've been gearing up for this for a while to figure out how to do it. What it comes down to is that we basically gave project responsibility to the joint team—the people who were the experts and the people who were the builders both had responsibility for the development. There was a great deal of cooperation at that time. It was not a situation where you sometimes get into the case and people say "Well these are my requirements and I'm going to throw them over the fence to you in MIS and MIS will then do what they think they need to do and put it back over to the other side of the fence for an approval and then that will get written up—and back and forth and back and forth. This often happens when people get worried about who's going to be to blame if this fails and it becomes a huge contract negotiation in effect. What we did here was everybody accepted responsibility for the project and they worked and worked together very closely together and worked a lot of long hard hours, but they got the job done because the people who know how to do pricing and marketing and the people who know how to build software at MIS got together and did the project. And, of course, there was a lot of support from up in top management too because it was a priority project, so everybody got together and did it. Of course, we would have found it disconcerting had we failed but we also bit off a problem we knew we could solve.

In regards to user acceptance, there are about a hundred stories now about the roll out. We got good acceptance from the beginning from the people other than the direct experts we were working with. But probably the best story is about when we rolled it out in Chicago. There was a sales rep who was very skeptical—and reasonably so: I mean to him it was just one more system to learn. He sat down and started doing a price estimate and sort of looked at it and looked back and started over and did it again and then let one of our knowledge engineers read it over. I asked him how it worked and what the algorithms were and so on, and he looked at it and punched a few more buttons and then he jumped up and said "Oh my god! Oh my god!" and ran downstairs to get the Federal Express envoy to the quote where he made a mistake. The issue was not that he was bad and the issue was not that anybody is trying to be careless or anything like that, the issue is that when you have a support system you need to remember all this stuff and make sure that you have the very latest up-to-date rates and tariffs and that sort of thing. And that's a key point, because here we have a situation where if you talk to a lot of systems analysts they'll say well the stuff that's going to change a lot, the little bitty programs, just put them on a PC because they are easy to change and then they suddenly realize that because they are on the PC they have a logistical nightmare to maintain them. Here the stuff that changes all the time, the rates and tariffs, maybe the rules about how we do pricing, whatever, are right there and we can control them. When there is stuff out there in PCs, the terminal emulators, and the word processors and so on. So the way we've avoided a logistical nightmare and what we have done is now provided a broadband communications medium in a very real sense. This is another communications medium to keep those updates immediately available to the dealer.

In regards to user training, we've got a pretty good way of doing that. We have a very efficient group of people who can do that. In fact a fellow was specifically hired, was put in the position of making sure that the systems are very effective and so why interfere with something that works so very well. So we just try to fit right into that strategy. It's important that you fit into your corporate strategy and corporate way of doing things. We have come up with sort of our own set of documentation approaches for the expert systems technology and we have found some things about that. First of all, a lot of it really tends to be too specific because the different schools up to a point are similar if they have the same paradigms. If you look at most programming languages that we document, they really have very similar programming paradigms. If you look at the expert system shells they put a mix and match, several major paradigms and then every one of them usually has some little weird twist. So it has been very difficult to come up with a universal. But we are sort of getting there and you have some basics that work very well. We try to provide a foundation and a working standard by which we document our systems so they talk to each other and they have done a good job of trying to pull all these conflicting systems and documentation together.

User support services is about the same as anybody else— just find somebody to do it. You have to be able to dial a phone number. There are people at each of the functional groups (e.g., the DBA) who are familiar with products and the applications and there is somebody for each of our applications too.

For managers and expert system developers who are about to transition expert systems into their organization, there are three important rules to remember: (1) all parties involved in the expert systems project should have direct responsibility, (2) have support from appropriate levels in the organization; and (3) you need to rely on your people and "protect" them from day-to-day issues.

The following are comments from Dr. Lashon Booker, of the Navy Center for Applied Research in Artificial Intelligence (NCARAI) at the Naval Research Laboratory, on the development and implementation of NCARAI's Bayesian Reasoning Tool (BaRT):[*]

The original idea was to take some of the state-of-the-art ideas about uncertainty management in knowledge-based systems and make them more accessible to the people building knowledge-based systems. One of the problems that I ran across in talking to people doing applied work in target classification, and looking

---

[*] Printed with permission from Lashon Booker.

around in general, is that there is this real lack of understanding about how hard the uncertainty management issue is and lack of familiarity with what current theory can provide. So essentially BaRT was put together to implement some of the current theories and to make them accessible to people. The intended audience, was people in the Navy working on classification problems that were analogous to the ones that we had been working on, like NRL's radar division, Space Systems division, and people at other labs like China Lake. We've also had some interest from people in academia who are interested in having access to our implementation of uncertainty management algorithms for teaching purposes or building their own little shells or whatever, and some interest from other government agencies like NASA Ames out on the west coast.

We have been working on BART for about 2 or 3 years. We haven't had the kind of concentrated heavily-funded effort that FIS (Fault Isolation System at the Navy Center for Applied Research in AI) had. We have paid a lot of attention to the quality of the work.

In terms of usage and payoff, I think it's too early to comment on that. I know it's being field tested now in different sites.

Yes, it has been used. Our system can be used in a couple of ways. You can either use it stand-alone as a shell for developing your own knowledge-based system or you can use it as a component in some other system, where essentially you use some software that we've written to do the uncertainty management for you. And it was in that latter mode that MITRE has been beta testing BaRT for us on a intelligence analysis problem that was too classified for me to know about. But they've actually delivered a system that they're very happy with using BaRT.

So, you know the payoffs of that are obvious. We get brownie points for transitioning technology—there is a transition. And we have made efforts to get our views to other places in the Navy and maybe that's a little more difficult. There's some institutional problems in the Navy that have nothing to do with transitioning AI technology; they have to do with the way things work in the Navy. There's another problem which comes up and that's people, scientists in general, especially anyone who has any kind of math background, feel pretty comfortable with probability theory and don't see what the big deal is. Bayes Rule has been around for a long time and the biggest problem we've had with the Navy community is dealing with scientists in other disciplines who know a smidgen about AI and convince themselves that they know enough about AI. When they see something that has probability theory in it they really get self confident and say, "Oh, this is a piece of cake." The bottom line is that the examples I've seen of Navy people trying to use BaRT have been pretty bad. They really don't understand the technical issues involved in constructing a correct model of a domain. There is an assumption that just because BaRT offers you the opportunity to develop a semantically sound model that anything you do with it is going to be semantically sound and that's not the case. If you've got a probabilistic model that's inherently inconsistent, it's going to be inconsistent no matter what way you try to manipulate it. The main problem we've had is trying to get people to see that it's not enough just to use the system, it's not enough to understand your problem, you have to understand the fit between your problem and the system.

In terms of legal issues involving distribution of BaRT, it boils down to whether we would supply the source code to people who wanted BaRT. This is still an open issue, but we are probably inclined to make BaRT public domain software and supply the code and some user documentation to users of BaRT. We would be happy to discuss ideas about improving BaRT and fixing any bugs that surface, but we would leave it up to the BaRT user to essentially take BaRT and improve or augment the code to fit his application.

In terms of lessons learned about transitioning expert systems or expert system shells into an organization, a major lesson is that people should understand the technology involved. An education process is needed to get appropriate management and staff introduced and up to speed on AI/expert systems technology. Once this is done, then people in the organization will understand the advantages and limitations of the technology and will know better how to use it to their benefit.

Users must be educated and trained if they are going to accept and use a computer system [4]. And before training even takes place, there must be user involvement in all phases of analysis, design, and development of the application system [4].

The user's involvement is especially critical in the design of the user interface of the expert system. Good interfaces, critical to user acceptance, are the kind of ergonomic factors that motivate users to accept the expert system and are essential to the success of any software development, not just AI-technology-based solutions [14]. That is why about 50% of the expert system's development is spent on designing and building the user interface [14]. To the user, the interface is the application; therefore, it's important that it be effective [14].

There are some major impediments to getting the user involved in the development and training process. Gardiner [5] describes ten common reasons why individuals have negative attitudes toward new technologies [6]. These include [5]:

- Obsolescence—"The technology may replace me."
- Exploitation—"The technology may be used to exploit me."
- Privacy—"The technology may be used to invade my privacy."
- Technophobia—"The technology is vaguely threatening."
- Technophilia—"The technology may involve me too deeply."
- Dependence—"The technology may become a crutch."
- Overload—"The technology may generate too much information."
- Informediation—"The technology may depersonalize me."
- Media-as-message—"The technology may change me."
- Opportunity cost—"The technology may take too much time."

There are also concerns that affect training in terms of how we relate to computers. The United Kingdom's Medical Research Council conducted a study and found that the majority of people view the computer as "an alien creature, isolating the user, mocking him with images of the world and its resources, to which he must haplessly conform [7]." Granted with more people "growing up" with computers, this fear of using the computer (i.e., cyberphobia) has been greatly reduced since this study was performed. However, the trainer must be attuned to these factors when determining how to train the expert system users. The trainer should also know the composition of the target audience in advance and should involve, in the training process, the ability to integrate the new knowledge into existing job functions [8]. This is where on-the-job training can be very beneficial; employees are able to immediately and directly apply their newly acquired knowledge to their specific tasks [6].

TYPES OF TRAINING FOR EXPERT SYSTEMS USERS

Expert system developers must recognize the need for fitting the expert system into the human and organizational environment. As Chapnick states [12]:

> Focussing solely on narrowly specified technical issues when designing and building expert systems is also clearly shortsighted and often leads to systems ultimately doomed to failure, no matter how good the software is. Systems must fit into the human and organizational environments as neatly as they fit into their technical environments. People must use the systems we design, and they must use them effectively and happily; the best systems actively improve workplace quality for their users. Designing systems with the potential to be perceived as threatening, inarticulate, inaccurate, double-binding, inappropriate, or irrelevant is an exercise in futility. Unfortunately, these issues are often cursorily treated or considered outside the scope of the initial, technically oriented feasibility study; designers often table them until the system is just about ready to move into production, if they treat the issues at all.

The training for users of expert systems is not much different than that for users of other computer software. Typically, both formal "classroom" training and on-the-job coaching are required to reach the desired level of proficiency in using the expert system. It is important that system users learn exactly what they are to do in an initial training course, so that they learn right the first time [3]. The training course would provide users with the necessary hands-on skills to use the expert system. In designing effective training courses, keep the following points in mind [9]:

1. Keep the trainees active (skill can be best developed by doing, not just listening or reading).
2. Make use of repetition (practice makes perfect).
3. Make use of reinforcement (reward correct responses).
4. Have trainees practice in many different situations so that they are able to generalize.

5. Organize the presentation of information in some meaningful way.
6. Provide for learning with understanding.
7. Encourage divergent thinking (urge students to develop creative solutions and explore alternative solutions).
8. Consider the trainee's ability to learn (some people learn quickly, some learn slowly).

Training materials should be developed after written instructions. The trainer should write down objectives for each training module, and then produce materials and exercises to meet those objectives [3]. "Refresher training" should be given every six months to make sure correct procedures are followed and to alert the users to new modifications to the expert system. Almost all the major expert system shell vendors have formal developer/user classroom training. Intellicorp offers up to two weeks of training on how to use KEE (Knowledge Engineering Environment), its expert system development tool. Inference Corporation, The Carnegie Group, and other shell vendors have similar arrangements for training on how to use their expert system shells.

The formal training course could be offered through a variety of vehicles. These include [4]: learner-paced vendor-supplied courses; in-house seminars run by outsiders; internally developed in-house seminars; off-site vendor seminars. Continuing education and training are important factors in the development and retention of a highly skilled staff. A Booz, Allen and Hamilton study found that their company had a turnover rate of only 11 percent for professionals who received ongoing education and training versus a 52 percent turnover rate for those who did not [10].

After a formal training course is completed, people usually require on-the-job coaching for a period of time [3]. The Intellicorp people will even tell you that after you take their KEE course, you should call them for help when you get back to start using KEE on the job for your specific expert system application. Following any training process, it is vital for the individual to practice on the job in order to retain the newly acquired knowledge and skills and to avoid forgetting what has been learned [6]. It has not been uncommon for the trainee to return to work to find that he or she must work extensive hours to catch up; this extra time requirement can be perceived as a penalty for attending the training class [6]. Managers must be sensitive to this occurrence and should offer as much support as possible to enhance these transitions.

After any kind of training, there should be an evaluation stage to make sure that the trainees learned what they needed to know and to measure the effectiveness of the training program. Some people [3, 6] suggest having training/testing databases that allow system designers to see if newly trained users can really do what needs to be done. Samples of the most frequent and most difficult types of problems are given to each new user, who then performs a series of transactions. If a new user meets some predetermined performance objective, say 98% of the items done correctly, then he or she is ready to perform on the job [3]. Evaluation of the training program itself should also be conducted. Here, system designers should obtain the feedback, perhaps in the form of a questionnaire, to measure the effectiveness of the trainer, course material, presentation format, and other pertinent criteria.

At Du Pont, the secret to their AI/expert systems training is to "eliminate the magic and start simply" [11]. Du Pont trains approximately 500 to 600 staff members on expert systems development each year. According to Peacock-Gillooly of the Du Pont AI Task Force [11]:

> We show them what an expert system looks like by taking the magic out of it with hands-on training. I always like to give my classes a little model to work on. For example, how to decide where to go to lunch. It's something very simple, and a bit comical, but it gets the point across. If you have 20 people sitting in the classroom, everyone has to go to lunch in the Wilmington area, they have some rules of thumb to do that. It's something they all can relate to.

Du Pont uses a multi-media presentation to train their users on expert systems. Du Pont trainers incorporate lectures, videos, and many demos into their training classes. They let each trainee use some selected expert system shells in order to get hands-on experience in building and learning about expert systems. This training approach has proved extremely useful and Du Pont has over 200 expert systems in use.

CONCLUSIONS

One of the first important steps that a manager should follow in institutionalizing expert systems is to provide both formal classroom and on-the-job training. For the user to better accept and use the expert system, expert system developers should make sure to get the user involved during the design, development, and testing of the expert system. The expert system developer should incorporate the comments and feedback of the user during the expert system's construction process. Proper user training on how to work the expert system then must be provided. Ongoing training in terms of refresher courses and distribution of appropriate training materials and user documentation must also be provided to the expert system users.

As Beau Shiel of the Price Waterhouse Technology Center states [15]:

> For expert systems to gain acceptance, mechanisms must be found to establish their credibility. One such mechanism is latent in the process of building a knowledge-based system internally. The person who builds the system is likely to believe that it contains valuable knowledge, since that person has invested energy considering that knowledge, working with it, and understanding it. Following an internal development, there is left a residue of people inside the organization who believe the knowledge is valid, and who are prepared to act as advocates for it. Just like an individual, organizations become bonded to knowledge through articulating it. Rational or not, this builds belief in a system's expertise, and, fundamentally, it's why internally developed systems will always have much greater success than externally developed ones.

> The second mechanism that people can use, to convince themselves of the validity of the knowledge, is more traditional. It is to buy the knowledge-based system from the people they've always bought that sort of knowledge from in the past. From the buyers' point of view, if they buy knowledge from a reputable, established knowledge source in some area, they know that source can be relied upon to ensure that the knowledge is valid or, at worst, to defend and support them if it turns out not to be. This

tendency to rely on the established knowledge vendors will produce a fundamental shift in the marketing of knowledge-based systems: from companies that add value through technology to companies that add value by virtue of having, and being seen to have, knowledge and authority in the field concerned. In the financial area this will be the banks, insurance companies and the big accounting firms. In the field of engineering it will be the consulting engineers, and so on. In each case, the traditional sources of expertise will become dominant, since they are the people who have the credibility to market knowledge without providing crisp answers to those awkward questions about validation mentioned earlier, and for which there simply are no satisfactory technical answers right now.

REFERENCES

[1]   Liebowitz, J. and D.A. DeSalvo (eds.), *Structuring Expert Systems: Domain, Design, and Development*, Yourdon Press/Prentice Hall, Englewood Cliffs, NJ, 1989.

[2]   Liebowitz, J., *Introduction to Expert Systems*, Mitchell Publishing, Watsonville, CA, 1988.

[3]   Bailey, R.W., *Human Error in Computer Systems*, Prentice Hall, Englewood Cliffs, NJ, 1983.

[4]   Borovits, I., *Management of Computer Operations*, Prentice Hall, Englewood Cliffs, NJ, 1984.

[5]   Gardiner, W.L., *Public Acceptance of the New Information Technologies: The Role of Attitudes*, Information Society Project, Gamma, Universite de Montreal, McGill University, Montreal, Canada, Paper No. I-9, 1980.

[6]   Glazer, D.A., "Strategies for Managers to Reduce Employee Fear When Introducing a New Technology," in *Managing Artificial Intelligence and Expert Systems*, D.A. DeSalvo and J. Liebowitz, (eds.), Prentice Hall, Englewood Cliffs, NJ, 1990.

[7]   Peitu, M., "Making a Match Between Man and Machine," *International Management*, September 1979.

[8]   Rogoff, R.L., *The Training Wheel*, John Wiley, New York, 1987.

[9]   Hilgrad and Bowers, 1975.

[10]   "Ongoing Training," *Infosystem*, February 1982.

[11]   Dunkerley, J., "Secret to AI Training: Start Simply," *Applied Artificial Intelligence Reporter*, University of Miami, Coral Gables, Florida, June 1987.

[12]   Chapnick, P., "Expert Systems and People," *AI Expert*, Miller Freeman Publications, San Francisco, CA, July 1989.

[13]   Colgrove, D. W., "Dummies Need Not Apply," *Infosystems*, ABC Publishing, New York, November 1987.

[14]   Chapnick, P., "Real People, Real Applications," *AI Expert*, Miller Freeman Publications, San Francisco, CA, June 1989.

[15]   "Interview with Beau Shiel," *International Journal of Computer Applications in Technology*, Inderscience Enterprises, Geneva, Switzerland, Vol. 2, No. 3, 1989.

CHAPTER 6

USER DOCUMENTATION GUIDELINES FOR INSTITUTIONALIZING EXPERT SYSTEMS

Expert systems user training is one important component of institutionalizing expert systems. Another equally critical part of the institutionalization process of expert systems is good expert system user documentation. Many wonderfully designed expert systems may not be used if the user documentation is poorly written. The manager should make sure that the expert system development group produces proper expert system user documentation. This chapter presents some guidelines for accomplishing this task.

WHY USER DOCUMENTATION IS IMPORTANT

Good documentation is an important part of the package in delivering an expert system. Inadequate user documentation causes at least five problems [1]:

- Human errors.
- Rejection of systems or programs.
- Wasted time and equipment.
- Increased training costs.
- Possible legal proceedings.

The major effect of poor user documentation is rejection of the expert system. Insufficient user documentation can strongly increase human errors in computer systems. Bailey [2] found that of all the human errors within the control of the software or computer designer, fully 60 percent of these were directly affected by the quality of the documentation efforts. User documentation is especially critical to the infrequent user of the expert system who might need to refer to some written instructions periodically on how to work the system.

   After recognizing the importance of good user documentation, the next step is to look at how expert systems differ from traditional software. This will influence the development of the associated expert system user documentation.

EXPERT SYSTEMS AND TRADITIONAL SOFTWARE FROM A USER DOCUMENTATION VIEWPOINT

Expert systems differ from conventional software in several ways that affect the complexity of user documentation. First, expert systems development typically involves rapid prototyping. Because expert systems are often developed from prototypes that are enhanced as they evolve, the corresponding development cycle for expert system documentation must be able to incorporate changes as they occur [3]. Second, unlike most other software, which presents the user with only one view of the system at a time, expert system software generally has "windowing" capability. This allows the user to have more than one view of the system at a time, which could increase confusion and frustration for a less experienced user [3]. Third, languages used to develop expert systems allow expert system developers to produce programs which are object-oriented and highly graphical. Traditional computer software has been largely textual and sequential, whereas expert systems may require documentation that uses an increased number of screen images to support the text [3]. Documentation efforts for expert systems should adhere to proven guidelines at the same time as they focus on the increased complexity that expert systems introduce. The ultimate goal must be functionality for end users [3].

McGraw [3] feels that the expert system user characteristics must be taken into account when developing the user documentation. Specifically, expert system users generally share the following traits:

- They do not necessarily have previous computer experience.
- Because expert systems are often used to assist novices, users are not usually experts in the domain that the expert system represents.
- Users need to retrieve information or advice from the expert system in an efficient, timely manner; the sophistication of the system itself should not inhibit ease of use.
- Expert system users tend to think of the expert systems as 'seamless'; that is, they are generally unaware of the individual components, displays, or knowledge bases which interact to make up the expert system.

While keeping these expert system user characteristics in mind, guidelines can be established for developing the user documentation.

GUIDELINES FOR EXPERT SYSTEM USER DOCUMENTATION

McGraw [3,4] outlines some important guidelines for developing expert system user documentation:

1. Develop a user profile.
2. Acquaint yourself with all available documents describing system functionality and design.
3. Complete a task analysis and an initial outline for your document.
4. Draft a design document that describes the implementation of human factors design issues.

5. Assign writers or teams to chapters, coordinate production schedules, and distribute the design document.
6. Write, edit, and internally test the document.
7. Determine external testing procedures, coordinate acceptance testing, and incorporate subsequent revisions.

Step one is necessary in order to understand the documentation's target audience. This will have an impact on the design of the documentation, and will also establish the users' previous experiences with computer systems and documentation [3]. Once this step is accomplished, the documentation developers should look at the system's functional design documents to get an overall view of its functionality. Then a task analysis should be performed that describes the tasks the user must be able to complete in order to use each segment of the system. Based upon this information, the documentation developers should build an initial outline for the user documentation [3].

Once the outline is made, the next step involves drafting a design document that describes the implementation of the documentation's design and style issues. The writing style, standards, typographical cues, spatial cues, and the standard layout for all chapters are factors that need to be considered. Then, writers are assigned chapters in the user documentation and the writers should meet with the designer of that portion of the expert system to determine the completeness and consistency of the design document [3]. Once the preliminary draft of a chapter has been completed, editing then commences and, following revisions, internal tests are made on that chapter. Someone other than the original writer and designer should use the chapter with the system, testing the accuracy, flow, and comprehensibility of the writing [3].

Upon completion of the individual segments of the user documentation, indexes and tables of contents may be completed [3]. Then, external testing can commence on the documentation. Testing with actual users can begin, whereby they use the manual as a guide while working with the system. Additionally, attitude surveys could also be used to measure users' attitudes of the documentation after an assigned task has been completed [3]. Finally, comments from the users involved in the testing are incorporated into the user documentation. Down the road, later revisions of the user documentation will be released.

CASE STUDY: FIESTA*

The following case involves expert system documentation [5]:

The purpose of the Fault Isolation Expert System for TDRSS (Tracking and Data Relay Satellite System) Applications (FIESTA) is to automate fault isolation and service monitoring for the Space Network. The Space Network provides NASA's primary means of communication with satellites and the Space Shuttle.

In terms of FIESTA's supporting documentation, it was recognized that the following documentation was important for the on-line operation of FIESTA:

- Implementation plan.
- Transition plan (from stand-alone prototype to on-line testbed).
- Functional requirements document.
- Systems requirements document.
  —Conventional format for interfaces and algorithmic processing.
  —Modified format for expert system component.
- Systems design document.
  —Same distinction as for Systems Requirements.
- Users manual/operational scenarios.
- Operations concept for the on-line testbed.
- Evaluation criteria.

Configuration management was also identified as a necessary element of deployment in an operational environment.

Design documentation. Even though there was no explicit design stage in the development of the FIESTA expert system component, it was decided to document the design of the prototype. By

*Reprinted with permission from Telematics and Informatics, Vol. 6, Nos. 3/4, N. Happell, S. Miksell, and C. Carlisle, "Expert System Development Methodology and the Transition from Prototyping to Operations: FIESTA, A Case Study," 1989, Pergamon Press plc. and the authors.

documenting the design, its maintenance could be facilitated. It was also found that in the effort to document the design, the system could be cleaned up, thus restoring most of the integrity which had been lost by numerous reworkings. The methods used to document the design helped identify areas that needed to be cleaned up and facilitated the restoration.

Structure Charts.   When working with a knowledge base the size of FIESTA (600 + rules), the easiest thing to lose track of is the rule interactions. The rules most likely to interact in FIESTA are those which are related functionally. Therefore, functionally related rules were kept together in the source code. However, with several developers working on the system over several years and many modifications to the system, it was inevitable that these groupings became less and less cohesive over time.

Structure charts were used showing the functional hierarchy of FIESTA to help restore these groupings. In the process of shuffling rules, redundant rules were identified, and rules which could be generalized to cover a higher-level function. Therefore, the number of rules was cut down. In addition, we used codes to indicate which lower-level functions represented individual rules, and which higher-level functions represented different types of files of source code, and placed these indicators in the appropriate structure chart boxes. As a result, the structure charts can be used as a table of contents to the source code, identifying which functions are performed, and exactly which rules perform them. Therefore, the structure charts can be a valuable tool for future maintenance.

Rule-relation Lists.   It was determined that a utility built into the expert system building tool (ART by Inference Corp. was used) provided an excellent means of keeping track of rule interactions. ART keeps a list of all rules, and another list of fact relations (generic fact formats). These lists are cross-referenced, so that the developer can view all of the rules which either reference a relation (using that relation as a pattern on their left-hand side), or assert facts defined by that relation into the knowledge base on the rule's right-hand side. These lists are useful in many ways, and can serve some of the same functions as data flow diagrams.

First they identify rules which could potentially impact one another. If a modification is made to a relation in one rule, the rule relation list can be referenced to identify which other rules may be affected by that change. Secondly, they can be used to help prevent superfluous facts from being asserted into the knowledge base. If there is a relation which has no rules which reference it (use it on the rule's left-hand side), then all of the rules which assert facts defined by that relation are adding information to the knowledge base which is never used. Likewise, useless rules can be identified by examining relations which have no rules to assert facts of that type. If these facts are not asserted at system initialization, all of the rules which reference that relation will never fire because no facts of that type are ever asserted.

Viewpoint Structure. The third most critical tool used to document the expert system design was a mapping of relations to viewpoints. Viewpoints are ART-provided utilities which allow the developer to partition the knowledge base into related areas. Each relation was defined to be used at different levels of the viewpoint network. Asserting or retracting a fact from the wrong viewpoint level could have major and unexpected effects on the program's execution. This documentation most closely parallels the documentation of a database design.

Although standard waterfall model methods of design documentation could be applied to FIESTA, means were established to document the design which served many of the same purposes. This documentation should aid in future maintenance efforts and help to retain the integrity of the system.

Configuration Management. Configuration Management (CM) was employed in an informal manner throughout the FIESTA life cycle. Directories are associated with each of the Builds (and sub-Builds), and changes within files have been documented with comments in the preface describing the modifications and when they were made, as well as identifying the responsible individual(s). This approach will be further formalized for operational use to assure that the following key requirements of CM are satisfied:

- Identification and availability of all source code corresponding to the operational system.
- Clearly defined procedures for introducing and tracking changes in the system (i.e., a complete audit trail).
- The ability to revert to an earlier version of the system.

Furthermore, CM will operate in conjunction with Quality Assurance Procedures (modified for rapid software development) to maintain a viable, dependable product. Central to the CM approach is the logging of all update procedures and the use of existing utilities to identify and archive files.

Summary.   Many of the features, milestones, and particularly documents which characterize the Waterfall Model are important for the effective development, implementation, and maintenance of a computer-based system. Generation of such documentation and the specification of milestones similar to those found in the Waterfall Model have characterized the transition of FIESTA from prototype to operations. Even though adaptation has been required to accommodate expert system technology, the intent of the documentation and the various reviews correspond closely to that associated with conventional software systems.

CASE STUDY: A Look at the Documentation for the Space Shuttle Onboard Navigation Console Expert/Trainer System (ONAV) [6]

The Onboard Navigation (ONAV) software system at NASA's Johnson Space Center (JSC) is for use in enhancing operational performance as well as training ground controllers in monitoring onboard Space Shuttle navigation sensors. The purpose of the ONAV system is to estimate the Space Shuttle Orbiter's position and velocity, and to recommend actions to improve or maintain navigation accuracy. Development of the rules for the ONAV system are generated and documented as four separate knowledge bases corresponding to each mission phase. The expert system incorporates the concept of modular design to logically partition both data and rules in order to promote and enhance program development and extensibility. CLIPS is used as the expert system shell for the development of ONAV [6].

Documentation.   The following documentation is used for ONAV [6]:

1. Expert system software code: The expert system software includes comment text, to the maximum extent practical, according to proposed documentation standards for expert systems

being developed at the JSC. Further, the comments are enhanced through the use of long, descriptive variable names, labels, and so on.

2. Guidelines and system requirements: This document is a top level overview of the ONAV development effort. This information is critical to providing proper direction to the project. Availability of this information not only provides a means to communicate to others not involved in the project, but also serves as a historical document. For very complex and detailed efforts, such a document serves as the first step in maintaining traceability and configuration control of software products.

3. Knowledge requirements: The target audience for this document is the knowledge domain expert. It is a reflection of "what the system knows" in a form as close as possible to the expert's language.

4. Design: This document is intended for use by the implementers of the expert system and serves as a guide for the coding effort. Contents include such things as fact formats, data representation, rule groupings, control flow, execution flow, interfaces, and so on.

5. User's guide: The user's guide presents procedures for preparation, operation, monitoring, and recovery of the expert system. The user's guide is based upon the design specification and is intended for the specific use of the users. It includes procedures for system operation directly in support of operational tasks.

6. Test plan: The test plan defines the total scope of the testing to be performed. It identifies the particular levels of testing and describes the contributing role for ensuring the reliability and acceptance of the system. It identifies the degree of testing and the specific functions that are involved in the tests. The test plan is for reviewing and ensuring that the technical requirements are met.

CONCLUSIONS

Documentation for expert system users is a critical part of the expert system institutionalization. User documentation serves to guide the user in how to work the expert system. Online tutorials are a means of adding to, rather than duplicating, any supporting print training materials [1]. By having adequate user documentation, this will hopefully encourage the user's interest in utilizing the expert system (that is, assuming the expert system is well tested and incorporates good human factors design).

REFERENCES

[1]   Brockmann, R. J., *Writing Better Computer User Documentation: From Paper to Online*, John Wiley, New York, 1986.

[2]   Bailey, R. W., *Human Error in Computer Systems*, Prentice Hall, Englewood Cliffs, NJ, 1983.

[3]   McGraw, K. L., "Guidelines for Producing Documentation for Expert Systems," *IEEE Transactions on Professional Communications*, IEEE, New York, December 1986.

[4]   McGraw, K. L., "Guidelines for Developing Expert Systems Documentation," in *Structuring Expert Systems: Domain, Design, and Development*, J. Liebowitz and D. A. DeSalvo (eds.), Yourdon Press/ Prentice Hall, Englewood Cliffs, NJ, 1989.

[5]   Happell, N., S. Miksell, and C. Carlisle, "Expert System Development Methodology and the Transition From Prototyping to Operaions: FIESTA, A Case Study," *Telematics and Informatics*, Vol. 6, Nos. 3/4, Pergamon Press, New York, 1989.

[6]   Wang, L., D. Bochsler, and L. Houston, "Space Shuttle Onboard Navigation Console Expert/Trainer System," *Proceedings* of SOAR '87 Conference, NASA Johnson Space Center, Houston, TX, 1987.

CHAPTER 7

USER SUPPORT SERVICES FOR INSTITUTIONALIZING EXPERT SYSTEMS

Besides providing training and documentation, it is very important in the expert system institutionalization process to provide the user with support services in case questions arise relating to the system's usage. Studies of end-user computing stress the importance of the support provided to users [1]. These user support services can come in a variety of forms. Most of these services are applicable to any software institutionalization, not just expert systems. This chapter will take a look at some of these user support services.

GOOD CUSTOMER SUPPORT

There are various vehicles to provide the expert system user with support and promote goodwill among the users. One common method is to have a hotline, typically a toll-free number that users can call to obtain answers to questions regarding the usage of the expert system shell or find out how to work the resulting expert system. Many organizations will provide user support delivered through a special organizational unit—an information center or a user support group—although in organizations wherein user development application is immature, it may be supported informally via personal contacts between users and individuals in the data processing departments, or between experienced and novice users [1]. The information center idea has been a popular approach for disseminating information on software usage. Many user groups have been formed in order to exchange ideas and information on particular hardware and software. The user group can serve as a catalyst for promoting new ideas relating to the use and enhancement of the expert system. Another way of providing good user support is to incorporate the comment of the users into future revisions of the expert system. Later releases of the expert system should be sent to each user and if the users see that their comments have been incorporated into the new releases, then this creates a positive attitude about using the expert system.

From the expert system developer's viewpoint, there are support services that are offered by shell vendors that could influence the shell selection process for expert system development. The issue of training on working the shell and having an available hotline for answering questions are important considerations in selecting a shell, if a shell is to be used. Additionally, some vendors offer knowledge engineering consulting as a support service when you buy the shell. This knowledge engineering consulting might last up to three days in order to help the customer when developing his/her (first) expert system. This support service might greatly influence one's shell selection. Another important consideration in terms of support services that the expert system developer needs to take into account is the question of whether the vendor will be around three to five years from now. Several expert system companies, like Palladian Software and Lisp Machines Inc., have come and gone. To provide future releases of the shell and adequate support services, the company needs to have a viable future.

A vehicle for enhancing user support services is to form a user group. A user group consists of individuals who are using the expert system, or expert system shell, and who get together on a regular basis to discuss their applications, new ideas, and provide some technology transfer. User groups can be a powerful means for keeping the change process progressing in a vital manner [3]. As Bouldin [3] points out, there are many benefits to forming user groups, including:

- The group provides an effective means for obtaining information.
- It offers a vehicle to communicate your opinions, beliefs, and experiences to a large audience.
- There will be opportunities for beginners to learn from the experts.
- A user organization can establish a channel for sharing associated products, such as user-supplied software.
- The sharing that takes place can include unresolved problems users encounter.
- The group can present a strong, united voice to the vendor.

Many expert system shell vendors have user groups that meet on a regular basis. In this manner, the vendor keeps in touch with its "clients" and obtains direct feedback from users about how to improve their product. For example, Exsys, Inc. sponsored an Exsys users conference so users of the Exsys shell could gather and discuss their applications. Officials from Exsys Inc. also discussed and gave tutorials of some of the latest features in the new version of the Exsys shell.

In a similar fashion, it might be advantageous to have a user group for a particular expert system. Since the expert system needs to be maintained anyway, the team performing this maintenance function could receive input from the system's users, for improving the system. The users might also enjoy learning from and interacting with other users.

As Huntington [4] explains:

> Texas Eastman Kodak's major effort to get end-user support, which included an in-house training program that quickly taught users how to build expert systems, succeeded in convincing users that an expert system is a helpful tool, not a job threat. In only two years, Texas Eastman fielded over 200 process control expert systems. Although most individual systems are small, the total collection represents well over 10,000 rules, containing knowledge of a vast number of plant operations.

The following are comments from William Spears, Navy Center for Applied Research in Artificial Intelligence, Naval Research Laboratory, on the Fault Isolation System (FIS).*

Troubleshooting in general takes a lot of time, effort, and *money*. For many new unit under tests (UUT), there is not much technician experience. Thus, it is hard to find people to write symptom–cause rules (global rules). It is also usually not feasible to fully simulate UUTs (i.e., Ohm's Law). FIS chooses an intermediate local representation (using qualitative rules) that is easier for people to determine. FIS derives the global behavior from the local rules.

There is a lot of interest in troubleshooting human engineered systems—important for fault detection and isolation. Also, there is a lot of interest in "design for testability" (i.e., designing right from the start systems that can be efficiently fault diagnosed). FIS could be adapted to such interests. Specifically, the major interest comes from people debugging electronic systems—the generation of test program sets (fault isolation programs) is very important to the Navy and industry.

FIS can be used as (or be adapted for use as) a technician's aid during fault isolation, a test tree generator (test program sets), and a testability evaluator. So far only the first two issues have been addressed. FIS is an advanced research prototype. It has been developed over seven years. Although it is fairly complete, there are still a few forms of diagnostic reasoning that need to be incorporated. FIS has been used by a number of beta test sites and private industry. FIS is still in the evaluation phase.

To get FIS accepted by the user community, the FIS developers asked for types of commands and features the community wanted. They contributed to both the definition and solution of the problem. This resulted in certain editors and various reasoning mechanisms as well as defining the knowledge actually used by the system. Also, their input resulted in the use of heuristics for best test strategies, as opposed to the more formal (but unexplainable) entropy strategies.

The following user training strategies for FIS were used: in-house tutorials, formal publications, and a collection of documentation. There were a series of guides describing the diagnosis and

* Printed with permission from William Spears.

knowledge acquisition subsystems. A written tutorial is still needed. For user support services, the FIS group supports the occasional phone call and in-house visits. Also, an arpanet address is available for correspondence.

FIS is being maintained across a number of platforms (SUN and ISI workstations, Symbolics Lisp Machine) running Common Lisp (or some variant) under UNIX (different versions). All of these can cause problems. It is very hard to maintain the software when hardware/software changes frequently.

Looking at legal/distribution issues relating to FIS, it is possible to patent or license FIS. Both routes involve some money to the authors. It is not clear yet as to the advantages and disadvantages of both routes. For distribution, at this point, we give binary only to industry. We give source code to the government and academic installations. If they want updates, they need to ask— we do not periodically send updates.

Some general advice for transitioning expert systems into an organization: (1) You need a competent program manager, system implementor, and support people for proper transitioning of expert systems; and (2) You need the program manager to decide some of the preceding issues, a system programmer to actually code up an efficient program, and support personnel to handle documentation, code distribution, phone calls, requests for information, and so on.

IMPORTANT LESSONS LEARNED ABOUT AI AND USER ACCEPTANCE

Eliot [2] describes some interesting lessons that affect the development, implementation, and user acceptance of AI. These lessons, as discussed earlier, are important to remember [2]:

- Don't do an AI project just because your competition does. First, determine that AI technology makes sense in your firm on its own merits.
- AI is a changing technology. Just because you started on Lisp machines doesn't mean that PC-based systems aren't useful and can't be integrated into your environment.

- Examine your current technological infrastructure and corporate culture, and pick an AI strategy that matches.
- The benefits of expert systems are more than just bits of software.
- AI is not magic.
- An AI system that produces economic benefit, but does not achieve its goals, may not be a failure.
- Have a portfolio of AI strategies.
- Don't be afraid to work with vendors or users in allied or even competitive industries.
- AI technologies create new dependencies that could boomerang. Consider the expert system that falls into a competitor's hands, the expert system vendor who goes out of business, or the knowledge engineer who quits.
- To believe that AI is the sole method for solving problems is to be possessed by the technology, and leads to failure.

By recognizing these lessons, the AI/expert systems project will have a strong likelihood of success in terms of development, implementation, and user acceptance.

CONCLUSIONS

Managers should recognize the "added value" of providing user support services for the expert system under use. The support services are a necessary part of the user acceptance process. Without adequate facilities for answering user questions, the expert system may be doomed to failure.

REFERENCES

[1]   Rivard, S. and S. L. Huff, "Factors of Success for End User Computing," *Communications of the ACM*, Association for Computing Machinery, New York, May 1988.

[2]   Eliot, L., "Case Studies in AI," presentation at the Second Annual

Software Development Conference, Miller Freeman Publications, San Francisco, CA, February 1989 (described in T. Schwartz, "Software Development '89 Covers All the Bases," *IEEE Expert*, IEEE, Los Alamitos, CA, Summer 1989).

[3]   Bouldin, B. M., *Agents of Change*, Yourdon Press, New Jersey, 1989.

[4]   Huntington, D., "Real Time Process Control Expert Systems Implementation Considerations," *AI Review*, American Assoc. for Artificial Intelligence, Menlo Park CA, 1989.

CHAPTER 8

MAINTENANCE STRATEGIES FOR INSTITUTIONALIZING EXPERT SYSTEMS

Maintenance is a key issue in institutionalizing expert systems. If the expert system is not maintained, then it will not continue to be used. The life cycle of an expert system does not end once it is implemented. Maintenance must be conducted on a continual basis after the expert system is implemented. A medical diagnosis expert system must be maintained to incorporate any new medical findings. A contracting expert system must be maintained to include new contract rulings and regulations. A tax expert system must be maintained to reflect any new tax laws. This chapter will look at some maintenance issues and strategies for expert systems.

THE IMPORTANCE OF SOFTWARE MAINTENANCE

Studies indicate that in business mainframe environments [1,2,3]:

- Programmers spend more than half of their time on maintenance.
- Software maintenance consumes as much as two-thirds of the total life cycle resources.
- Software applications may cost as much as 200 percent more to maintain than to develop.

The more complex a program, the more maintenance is required. In expert systems, maintenance is needed because new knowledge must be entered into the system, and outdated or incorrect knowledge must be updated and replaced, respectively. CATS-1, General Electric's internal system for diagnosing problems with diesel locomotive engines, had to be shelved because the company couldn't maintain the structure it created for such expert systems [4]. CATS-1 faded into oblivion because of poor planning and improper maintenance guidelines [4].

Software maintenance is the performance of those activities required to keep a software system operational and responsive after it is accepted and placed into production [5]. There are three types of software maintenance: perfective, adaptive, and corrective. Perfective maintenance includes all changes, insertions, deletions, modifications, extensions, and enhancements which are made to a system to meet the evolving and/or expanding needs of the user. Adaptive maintenance consists of any effort which is initiated as a result of changes in the environment in which a software system must operate. Corrective maintenance refers to changes necessitated by actual errors (induced or residual "bugs") in a system [5]. Software maintenance represents 60% to 70% of the total cost of software which runs into the tens of billions of dollars each year [5]. Perfective maintenance comprises approximately 60% of the software maintenance costs; adaptive maintenance and corrective maintenance are each approximately 20% of the total [5].

With the costs associated with software maintenance, one can easily see that good software design is important in order to reduce some of these costs. This is just as true with expert system software. Studies [1] have shown that structural differences do impact maintenance performance. Specifically, improving a system by eliminating GO TOs and redundancies through writing procedures at the highest level possible appears to decrease the time required to perform maintenance, and to decrease the frequency of ripple effect errors [1]. Kapur [6] cites some of the present factors contributing to the problems of software maintenance. These include: (1) data processing management devotes little effort to solving the software maintenance problem; (2) new tools and methodologies are mostly used for development; (3) there is a lack of high quality staff in the software maintenance department; and (4) there is a belief that software engineering techniques are not applicable to software maintenance. Ramamoorthy et al. [7] cite other problems associated with software maintenance. These include: (1) insufficient or incomplete documents, (2) inconsistency between the documents and the code, (3) design difficult to understand, modify, and test, and (4) insufficient record of past maintenance. Wong [8] suggests that the major causes of software maintenance problems are the growth of the inventory of software which must be maintained, and the failure to adopt and utilize improved technical and management methods, techniques, and tools for developing quality software.

MAINTENANCE STRATEGIES FOR EXPERT SYSTEMS

One way to provide adequate maintenance for expert systems is to improve user knowledge. Lientz [9] in a study administered to data processing managers found that the lack of user understanding and inadequate user training account for the majority of the variance in data processing management's assessment of the problems in software maintenance. This result provides further evidence of the importance of the relationship between the users and the providers of information systems in the determination of system success or failure.

One advantage that expert systems have over some other software is that their development typically involves rapid prototyping. Rapid prototyping facilitates the interaction and incorporation of comments between the users and the expert system developers. This "build a little, test a little" approach allows users to comment on each version of the expert system prototype, thus facilitating improved user knowledge. By allowing users to get actively involved in the expert system development process, the expert system developer should be able to design the system to better meet users' requirements and thus reduce some later problems in maintaining the system.

A second way of improving expert system maintenance is to adopt a reusable software approach. Reusable software is defined as the reuse of any information that may be collected and later used to develop the software [8,10]. Reusable software is an underlying goal when expert system developers use expert system shells. The use of expert system shells can greatly reduce the amount of expert system maintenance (as opposed to developing an expert system from scratch) because the shell part of the expert system, namely the inference engine and dialog structure, have already been thoroughly tested and maintained on an ongoing basis. This should reduce the margin of error associated with design problems that could lead to increased expert system maintenance problems.

The following are comments from Dibble and Bostrom [15] on expert system maintenance:

> The expert system maintenance problem may differ from that in traditional systems because all necessary changes will not be driven by program problems or additional desired functionality. The nature of a knowledge base is that it is constantly changing; experts are constantly updating their knowledge. Important questions are: How quickly do real domains change, and at what cost to the knowledge base? and What techniques can be used to induce some stability to an evolving knowledge base? Sridharan suggests perhaps keeping libraries of examples or domain archetypes. Certainly, the operational expert systems have required significant postinstallation support, so the estimation of maintenance effort is worthy of attention.

Some software managers do not adopt a reusable software approach for several reasons [10]:

- If no tools or components exist, then it will take time and manpower to create the tools and components, and to gain the expertise in their use. Such costs are generally not within the budget of a single project.
- If special tools (e.g., application generators, and so on) are

used to create a program, then a customer might expect these tools to be delivered along with the product for maintenance purposes.

- If the tools do exist for making programmers more productive, then this will make the project dependent on fewer personnel. Any reduction in staff might be perceived as reducing the manager's "empire."

- If a defect appears in a program developed using reused components, who is legally responsible for damages?

- If there are no standards to control what is entered into the reusable components library, then time and money must be spent setting and maintaining the standards for the library.

In spite of these possible viewpoints, many people are recognizing that software reuse, if possible, can greatly save in development and maintenance time and costs. This seems to be a positive step in developing expert systems using shells.

Another important guideline in maintaining expert systems is to have a structured methodology to facilitate the maintenance of the expert system. A good case in point is XCON, Digital Equipment's expert system used for configuring VAX computer systems. XCON is one of the largest expert systems, with over 10,000 rules. It is anticipated that DEC's configuration systems can have upwards of 20,000 to 30,000 rules in the near term [11]. There has been a team of about 15 persons assigned to maintain XCON. To aid in this process, a software methodology called RIME [12] has been developed to help build and maintain very large configuration systems. XCON was reimplemented utilizing RIME and the new implementation has been in production use since January 1988. RIME is used to better manage the size, complexity, and quantity of XCON's rules. Developers using RIME can use three forms of control: algorithmic control, if the task they are implementing can be accomplished through a sequence of steps with little variation; situation recognition, if the conditions and actions are straightforward and limited; and deliberate decision, if there are complex situations with many variations and interactions [12]. The main benefit of having a structured methodology like RIME for development, and ultimately maintenance, of an expert system is to have controlled growth and management so that the expert system does not become too unwieldy.

The XCON experience uncovered some important guidelines for facilitating maintenance of an expert system. These guidelines include [11]:

- Complex rules need to be broken down; in particular, multiple tasks need to be factored out and each task needs to be made into an explicit, separate process (for example, have a set of rules that accomplishes the task of selecting a device, a set of rules that accomplishes the task of selecting a container for another component, and another set of rules that accomplishes the task of selecting the particular location within the container to place the other component).
- Need to co-locate similar rules.
- Criteria for grouping should be explicitly identified and recorded in "subgroup schemes" (those schemes, much like database schemes, provide abstractions describing sets of rules that allow developers to efficiently index into the rule base).

Another strategy for maintaining expert systems is to keep a maintenance log of the changes that are made after implementing the expert system in the organization. By documenting the changes in the expert system as a result of perfective, adaptive, and corrective maintenance, this will serve as a base guide to the expert system maintainer in order to compare new changes with what was done previously in the system. Also, if the expert system maintainer leaves the organization, his or her replacement would use the maintenance log as part of the training material. Additionally, a Knowledge Engineer's Manual should be prepared which contains the knowledge base, links to other systems/databases, and other pertinent information for maintaining the expert system.

The last important strategy for maintaining the expert system is to designate a team of individuals whose job includes maintaining the expert system. The expert system is a "living, breathing creature," whose knowledge base will have to be updated and maintained frequently. Without a constant upkeep of the expert system, its knowledge will become "non-current" which will cause the expert system to fall into disuse.

CASE STUDY: Long-Term Maintenance of EXPERTAX: An Expert System for Aiding in the Corporate Tax Accrual and Planning Function*

EXPERTAX, developed by Coopers & Lybrand, is an operational expert system used for providing guidance and advice, through issue identification, to auditors and tax specialists in preparing the tax accrual for financial statement purposes [13]. Since expert systems utilize a knowledge base, and a knowledge base almost always requires updating and modification, expert system developers could spend increasingly more time modifying current systems rather than developing new ones [14]. This trend can be reversed if the expert system's architecture is developed in a way which allows the experts, not the developer, to update their own knowledge base [14]. A Knowledge Base Maintenance System (KBMS), developed by Coopers & Lybrand, provides a way for maintaining the expert system.

KBMS (not to be confused with AI Corporation's expert system development tool, KBMS) is described as follows [13,14]:

Knowledge base maintenance system.   A system that has an easy-to-use maintenance structure provides many advantages for those who must support it after its initial development. Most important, a system that is successfully maintained may lend itself to further corporate commitment because it continues to be a valuable asset.

The EXPERTAX knowledge base maintenance system is an independent software system designed to update, modify, and expand the knowledge base. The system includes a frame editor, logic evaluator, and rule interaction display.

The frame editor permits the user to state the different components of a frame in simple English. It edits the information entered for consistency and completeness and helps the user correct omissions or inconsistencies.

The logic evaluator checks for possible conflicts in logic between the rules in the frame being edited and the rules contained in cur-

---

*Reprinted with the permission of Learned Information (Europe) Ltd.

rently valid frames. If an inconsistency is discovered, the evaluator suggests editorial actions that would resolve the situation.

The rule interaction display allows the user to dynamically observe all the frames affected by changes in the frame being edited. This permits the user to better visualize changes in operating procedure that could be implicit in modifications of a frame with several complex rules or follow-up routines.

For future updates of EXPERTAX, at least one tax specialist is responsible for each of the 16 topic areas in EXPERTAX. Maintaining EXPERTAX also requires the full-time effort of the EXPERTAX knowledge base manager. In addition, QShell (the shell used to build EXPERTAX) requires the periodic attention of the knowledge engineer to provide enhancements to the user interface.

Scheduled periodic assistance is also required in the quality assurance and distribution phases for each release of the software. Each release requires considerable quality review by the firm's Auditing Directorate, checking for potential "bugs," logical inconsistencies, and the like. Feedback is provided to the knowledge base manager through a hotline number for users who have questions, comments, or suggestions.

Thus, EXPERTAX is supported by a knowledge base maintenance organization (KBMO), consisting of the periodic involvement by the individuals described who provide the support which any complex product or service needs. EXPERTAX does not require a lengthy user's manual (it comes with a summary card), so few writing, editing, and printing services are needed.

This organizational structure differs from accounts of other corporations currently supporting expert systems. Most often, companies create a self-contained expert system group responsible both for creating new programs and maintaining existing ones. There is mounting evidence that this type of organizational structure may lead to several long-term maintenance problems. First, knowledge engineers have a greater interest in creating new systems than in maintaining existing ones. Second, users and experts are in a better position to determine new directions an expert system should take than are those removed from daily use of and contact with the program.

Long-term maintenance costs.   Maintaining a system as complex as EXPERTAX involves expense. Reducing or eliminating the need for a knowledge engineer in the long-term maintenance function makes him or her available to create new systems. The experts will continue to be needed to provide current and revised information to the system, so this cost is relatively fixed.

Additional costs arise from hardware, customer service, installation, royalty costs, training and advertising/marketing. While hardly incidental, these costs are largely determined by the purpose and distribution of the system. Costs in several of these areas (e.g., hardware, customer support and training) can be eliminated or reduced by programming efforts during development. As a result, long-term costs will be reduced.

CASE STUDY: Maintaining an Expert Planning System: A Software Tools Approach*

Introduction and background.   The maintainability of any system is the degree to which quick changes can be made to it without disruption. Traditional software systems have required redesign, rewriting, and recompiling before they could be tested. Knowledge Based (KB) systems have allowed much quicker changes to systems by allowing the system engineer to edit, add, or delete KB structures. This is because KB systems have made certain parts of the system explicit and easily modifiable. Other parts of most KB systems, such as the user interface, remain hard to change. The software tools approach to system design defines an environment within which a system can be built through the use of tools which can more easily modify some of these other hard to change parts.

The planning system which is described here uses software tools in combination with the KB approach (the KB approach can be viewed as a tool) to allow easier maintenance of the entire system. The reader will notice that the overall task performed by the human scheduler is divided into a set of independent subtasks which use tools.

The Earth Radiation Budget Satellite (ERBS) has been using an expert planning system to schedule Tracking and Data Relay Satellite (TDRS) communications links since May, 1987. A product of this system is a set of reports called Schedule Add Requests (SARs) which are forwarded to the Network Control Center (NCC). The NCC, in turn, lets each user of the system know whether or not a specific

*Printed with permission from David McLean.

request is granted or rejected. Rejected requests must be resubmitted by using alternative scheduling strategies. This scheduling task can be broken into four subtasks.

1. Generation of viewing periods for TDRS east, TDRS west, spacecraft daylight, and orbit numbers.
2. Generation of a schedule from the viewing periods, a planning knowledge base and a user's input.
3. Generation of SARs and additional reports which allow the user to refine and validate the schedule.
4. Submission of the SARs to the NCC and obtaining feedback on the status of each request for TDRS contact.

The viewing periods (resource windows) are generated by software which reads an orbital data tape and which uses heuristics which describe when each of the resources are "in view" from the satellite's point of view. These heuristics include information on when the resources are occulted by the earth or by other satellite obstructions.

The bulk of the work in the next subtask is accomplished by a tactical planning tool called PARR (Planning and Resource Reasoning shell) [1] which was developed by Bendix Field Engineering Corporation for the National Aeronautics and Space Administration at Goddard Space Flight Center. This tool is a reactive planning shell which uses a strategic KB and resource windows to generate a schedule. The strategic KB is frame based and contains information about how to schedule the various activities as well as information to be used during conflict resolution such as:

1. When, how long, and how often an activity is to be scheduled.
2. Activity constraints.
3. Activity resources.
4. Alternative ways of scheduling the activity.
5. Activity priority, shiftability, and substructure.

Once the resource windows have been generated, PARR is invoked in a batch mode to generate the first cut of a weekly schedule. In the batch mode, PARR acts independently and consults a planning KB.

Next, PARR is invoked in an interactive mode so the mission scheduler (user) can interactively edit and fine tune the schedule. In the interactive mode, PARR acts like an intelligent assistant.

When the mission scheduler is satisfied with the schedule, a series of reports are generated which reflect the current state of the schedule. Among these reports will be the SARs which are submitted to NCC. As feedback is obtained from the NCC, subtasks 2 through 4 are repeated as required in order to satisfy all the constraints demanded by the NCC. At present, software tools are available for aiding subtasks 1 through 3. All of these tools are written in C and will run on IBM PC compatibles and UNIX-based workstations.

Maintenance of any system means responding to some kind of change which is imposed upon the initial requirements of the system. The evolution of the ERBS-TDRS scheduling system will now be described in terms of responses to three different areas of change:

1. User interface changes.
2. Task environment changes.
3. System enhancement and redesign.

User interface changes.   The ERBS-TDRS planning system was originally delivered with a manual which was organized by subtask and which specified how to invoke the scheduling tools in order to accomplish each subtask. After using the system for a time, each of these subtasks became more clearly defined and many of the more routine subtasks were implemented as script files (batch files) which could be invoked with far less interaction with the user. This evolution resulted from both user feedback and system redesign considerations.

The most dramatic change from the user's point of view was the addition of a menu system, called the Menu-Based Executive or MEX [2], which could indirectly invoke the low level tools and script files from the user's selection of menu options. Once the user became familiar with the menu system's use, the user's manual was never consulted again. Part of the reason for this was due to the refinement of context-sensitive help features but most of it was due to the logical organization which the menu hierarchy forced on the entire task.

Other features which made the task easier include:

1. Enhancing the schedule edit feature to allow the insertion of a new activity by graphic positioning.
2. Reformatting some of the reports [3] for better readability.
3. Enhancing the menu system to include a form-filling feature which allows form-filling via menu selection.

Notice that these changes are strictly user interface changes and that because the user interface is independent of the tools used to accomplish the overall task, these changes did not disrupt tool usage. Most important, note that the menu system can be viewed as a user-configurable (generic) user interface tool which can be used in any software tools application.

Task environment changes. From the very beginning, changes were imposed upon the system in terms of the types of activities to be scheduled. Because these activities are specified in a KB and because the representation used is both explicit and generic, changes of this type are very easy to make. Often, these changes were imposed for a temporary period of time due to testing requirements. When this was the case, a temporary subdirectory was set up and temporary KBs were defined and used as required.

Although the KB changes were easy to make, they did require the support of a systems (or knowledge) engineer who was familiar with the KB structure and syntax. In an effort to circumvent this requirement, a tool was developed which allows the user to generate new KBs by specifying activities through menu selection. This was done by first defining a grammar of menus which defined the domain of activities in terms as generic as possible. The tools which resulted from this effort are known as Plan Specification Tools (PST) [4]. PST allows a planner to specify activities in terms of strategic plans which can then be executed by the tactical planner, PARR. Although PST still requires some knowledge of how the PST-PARR environment is put together, it greatly reduces the time required to develop new strategic KBs. Further, PST uses the same user interface code as does the menu system so that PST maintenance is greatly simplified.

Another area where the environment changed was in the communications resources which were available. When the system was first delivered, only TDRS east was available. Currently, both TDRS east and TDRS west are being used. This change required reading additional data from the orbital tape and generating new resource windows for the new resource type (TDRS west). The resource generation tool is specific to the ERBS application but was designed with this change in mind, so the effort to support this change was minimal. In addition, new activity types which described the use of this new resource had to be added to the strategic KB.

Finally, new menu options and tools were added to the system when the user decided that these features would be worthwhile. One such option was a feature which dumped a few of the records from the orbit tape to a printer so that a quick check could be made on the "validity" of the data. Another feature was an option for generating a report to be submitted to the NCC in order to request that a previously requested activity be deleted.

The ability of tools to anticipate change is fundamental to their successful use in any application. Editing tools which allow the system maintainer to make these changes easily and accurately are always welcome.

System enhancement and redesign.   The user interface enhancements of using script files and the menu system have had a major effect on the maintenance of the system. The menu system literally defines the major subtasks in terms of a top-down design hierarchy. The script files define the macros which use the low level tools to accomplish each component of the subtasks. In addition to independent files which contain data of a particular type such as KB files and input schedule files, there are also configuration files which list the various aggregate files to be used by a particular subtask. Configuration files thus further abstract system details so that various configurations can be managed easily. And thus maintenance amounts to browsing this system structure and changing or adding a component at the appropriate level (menu, script, configuration file, KB, tool, and so on).

Because PARR will also be used to support other missions, it has been evolving independently, but compatibly, with respect to the ERBS planning requirements. More sophisticated control procedures and conflict identification and resolution tools are constantly being added to PARR. In addition, the user interface features for PARR are evolving and have been implemented using a number of different interfacing libraries, including Curses and X-Windows. As noted earlier, a basic design effort for PARR is that of keeping the user interface portions as independent as possible from the rest of the system. This independence has allowed each portion to evolve independently and has greatly added to the ease of support during the evolution.

Increase in complexity is not the only direction of evolution. PARR's system engineers are always looking for ways to accomplish the same task by simpler and easier means. A major simplification was accomplished by eliminating the use of a backward chaining inference engine (TIE1) [5] which was used to do constraint checking. Simplifying this portion of the system resulted in eliminating the overhead of a needlessly complex set of procedures and data structures. It also resulted in the consolidation of multiple KBs with different representation schemes into one KB where all the activities are defined. Admittedly, each activity KB structure contains hybrid slot representation, but the overall effect of bundling everything into one structure in one KB greatly aids maintenance of the system. A system that has a great deal of diverse KB representation schemes may be sophisticated but it is harder to maintain.

Conclusions.   The formal KB portion of this system is relatively small and is currently the easiest to maintain. The term "formal" is used here because it is not exactly clear just where all the knowledge of this system resides. Certainly it takes knowledge to organize the overall task into manageable subtasks, each of which may provide output and input to other subtasks. Making the entire system explicit in structure and function has in effect made many other parts of the system appear as though they too were KB components. It is this explicitness of the system architecture that allows it to anticipate change. Thus, the number and types of different activities, resources, menu options, reports, and so on is not defined ahead of time, rather they each get redefined as the system evolves. In this respect, the system's architecture is like a language through which the system designer can express these changing task components. It is the combined properties of explicit structure and function as well as ease of change which makes the software tools approach to this planning system so manageable.

The use of tools to help the user accomplish a task is an old idea. However, the use of tools to make other tools easier to use (script files and menu systems) and also to change other tools (KB editors) is a relatively new idea. Keeping all these tools as independent as possible and applying each to clearly defined subtasks is a very important part of tool design and usage. Choosing the right tool for the right task is very difficult for the uninitiated and there are many instances of force fitting tools to tasks which end up as disasters. This is particularly true with the so-called inference engines which are described as being so general that they will solve anyone's problems.

Tools should always be defined by and in terms of the task when possible. Low level tools have the advantage that they are not specific to a particular task and thus they can be used as building blocks to build more specific tools which help accomplish specific tasks. High level tools have the advantage that they can be used as is or with little change but they are necessarily specific to certain classes of tasks. Maintaining a changing software system will therefore be aided by the degree to which the system engineer has access to the low level tools which allow the most flexibility.

The choice of the portable language C not only anticipates possible hardware upgrades but also makes these tools available to a large number of other users whose needs may be similar.

Acknowledgement.   This work was supported by NASA contracts NAS5-31000 and NAS5-27772. The author wishes to thank Patricia Lightfoot and Carolyn Dent at NASA-GSFC/Code 514 and Ellen Stolarik at Bendix Field Engineering Corporation for their continual support of this work.

PARR References

[1]   *PARR Knowledge Base Author's Manual.* NASA-GSFC/Code 514, March 1989.

[2]   *MEX: A Portable Menu-Based Executive.* NASA-GSFC/Code 514, November 1988.

[3]   *Generic Data Entry and Report Generation Tools.* NASA-GSFC/Code 514, February 1989.

[4]   McLean, D. R., Yen, W. L. "PST & PARR: Plan Specification Tools

And A Planning And Resource Reasoning Shell For Use In Satellite Mission Planning," *Proceedings* of the 1989 Goddard Conference on Space Applications of Artificial Intelligence, May 1989.

[5]   McLean, D. R., "The Design And Application Of A Transportable Inference Engine (TIE1)", *Telematics And Informatics*, Vol. 3, No. 3, 1986.

CONCLUSIONS

Maintenance is an important area for institutionalizing expert systems within the organization. A system whose knowledge is not updated would probably not be used, even if it's well designed. A contracting expert system or a legal expert system that does not reflect new rules, laws, and regulations may be useless to the user. In planning the design of the expert system, the developer needs to think of how it will be maintained. An appropriate maintenance methodology should be incorporated into the system to facilitate future maintenance. This chapter provided guidelines and strategies to make managers more aware of the importance of maintaining the expert system.

REFERENCES

[1]   Gibson, V.R. and J.A. Senn, "System Structure and Software Maintenance Performance," *Communications of the ACM*, Association for Computing Machinery, New York, March 1989.

[2]   Lientz, B.P. and E.B. Swanson, *Software Maintenance Management*, Addison-Wesley, Reading, MA, 1980.

[3]   Parikh, G., Tutorial on Software Maintenance, IEEE, New York, 1983.

[4]   Newquist, H.P., "Struggling to Maintain," *AI Expert*, Miller Freeman Publications, San Francisco, CA, August 1988.

[5]   Osborne, W.M., *Executive Guide to Software Maintenance*, NBS Special Publication 500-130, National Bureau of Standards, Gaithersburg, MD, October 1985.

[6]   Kapur, G., "Software Maintenance," *Computerworld*, September 26, 1983.

[7]   Ramamoorthy, C.V., A. Prakash, W. Tsai, and Y. Usuda, "Software
        Engineering: Problems and Perspectives," *Computer*, IEEE, October
        1984.

[8]   Wong, W., *A Management Overview of Software Reuse*, NBS Special
        Publication 500-142, National Bureau of Standards, Gaithersburg,
        MD, September 1986.

[9]   Lientz, B.P. and E.B. Swanson, "Problems in Application Software
        Maintenance," *Communications of the ACM*, Association for Comput-
        ing Machinery, New York, November 1981.

[10]   Wong, W., *Management Guide to Software Reuse*, NBS Special Publica-
        tion 500-155, National Bureau of Standards, Gaithersburg, MD,
        April 1988.

[11]   Barker, V.E. and D.E. O'Connor, "Expert Systems for Configuration
        at Digital: XCON and Beyond," *Communications of the ACM*, Associa-
        tion for Computing Machinery, New York, March 1989.

[12]   Bachant, J. and E. Soloway, "The Engineering of XCON," *Communi-
        cations of the ACM*, Association for Computing Machinery, New
        York, March 1989.

[13]   Shpilberg, D., L.E. Graham, and H. Schatz, "ExperTax: An Expert
        System for Corporate Tax Planning," *Expert Systems*, Vol. 3, No. 3,
        Oxford, England: Learned Information Ltd, July 1986.

[14]   Schatz, H., R. Strahs, and L. Campbell, "ExperTax: The Issue of
        Long-Term Maintenances" *Proceedings* of The Third International
        Expert Systems Conference, Oxford, England: Learned Information
        Ltd., 1986.

[15]   Dibble, D. and R.P. Bostrom, "Managing Expert Systems Projects:
        Factors Critical for Successful Implementation," *Proceedings* of the
        1987 ACM SIGBDP-SIGCPR Conference, New York: Association for
        Computing Machinery, 1987.

CHAPTER 9

LEGAL ISSUES AND ORGANIZATION ADOPTION/DISTRIBUTION STRATEGIES FOR EXPERT SYSTEMS INSTITUTIONALIZATION

To build, market, distribute, and institutionalize an expert system, the organization should be aware of some important legal considerations. For example, is the manufacturer of the expert system liable if the expert system produces faulty advice? Can the manufacturer of the expert system copy protect his or her expert system through copyrights and patents? Can the expert whose knowledge is in the expert system receive royalties each time a copy of the expert system is sold? Does the organization using the expert system need a site license to make multiple copies to distribute throughout the organization? Should the expert system be resident on a mainframe and then downloaded to terminals to protect it from being tampered with? Should the organization use the expert system on a personal computer (PC) and then make copies for the hundreds of users within the organization each time an updated version of the expert system is made?

All these questions are important to the expert system institutionalization process. Managers must be aware of possible legal entanglements resulting from expert system use, and should anticipate possible legal actions and protect themselves against these. Likewise, managers must think in advance of how the expert system is going to be distributed to the users within the organization. Managers must think about the kind of network capabilities that are needed within the firm to access the expert system. Do the managers want to transition the expert system to a separate organization to handle expert system updates and customer support? These types of questions must be answered in the minds of the managers in order to properly institutionalize the expert system. The earlier managers think about these questions, the easier it will be to safeguard against these possible problems.

This chapter looks at both legal issues and organizational distribution considerations pertaining to expert systems.

LEGAL ISSUES INVOLVING EXPERT SYSTEMS

The trend toward mass-marketed expert systems suggests that legal liability will become increasingly important [1]. Expert systems are being designed for the layperson to help draft wills, make contracts, diagnose children's health problems, and provide tax advice. What happens if the expert system incorrectly diagnoses a five-year-old's medical problem or the tax expert system gives advice which proves faulty after the taxpayer's IRS audit? Who is liable? This results in what lawyers call a "tort issue." At one end of the spectrum, total responsibility lies with the action taker, while at the other end, total responsibility lies with the producer of the advisory system [2]. One assumption which has been stated by expert system developers is that since someone must act on the results of the system's advice, the person taking action will always have full responsibility. This assumption has not been effective in comparable situations such as navigation charts, books, or medical diagnostic and monitoring equipment [2]. Therefore, it is unlikely that this approach will prove to be an effective defense in the case of expert systems.

It is quite possible that expert systems used in fields such as medicine, law, and accounting may well become subject to licensing requirements [3]. Already, medical expert systems come under the auspices of and are regulated by the Food and Drug Administration. Will an expert system that aids in controlling air traffic have to be licensed by the Federal Aviation Administration, just as a human controller is [3]? This situation may not be too farfetched. Of course, one sees the critical importance of thorough verification and validation of an expert system!

In the coming years, the next growth area for litigation relating to AI will be in liability, ownership, licensing, and patent infringement. The issue of liability is a major concern among expert systems developers. Because of the complicated relationship between the vendor and the user, allocating responsibility for such failures is by no means straightforward [3]. And failures there will almost certainly be; no complex computer program has ever been marketed that did not have some defect, somewhere [3]. The issue of ownership, that is protecting a program developer or producer, is guided by the service versus product distinction [4]. As Zeide and Liebowitz explain [4]:

> If a program is product, it is possible that it can be patented. However, this would require that it be deemed a novel invention, unique in the state of the art. It cannot be on the market for more than one year prior to the issuance of the patent. In addition, a patented product is usually a tangible item. But although programs are sold and transferred on physical discs, it is the content of the disc, not the disc itself, that is really the 'product.' For these reasons, developers usually go the copyright route for protection of their programs. This further substantiates the conflict of whether an expert system is a product or a service.

With the possibility for legal suits resulting from AI services and products, how can the AI developer protect himself from possible legal action? This will be explained next.

WAYS FOR THE AI DEVELOPER TO LIMIT HIS OR HER LIABILITY

First of all, the AI developer should use disclaimers in sales contracts to limit his or her liability against such things as misuse, or to warn the user regarding the output from the AI product [5,6,7]. For example, an expert system to help diagnose breast cancer might have a disclaimer stating that the conclusions reached by the system are not final and no matter what the findings, the user (i.e., the patient) should consult her doctor. In the event of incorrect advice, this disclaimer does not get the AI developer "off the hook," but a disclaimer may be used to perhaps limit his or her liability.

Second, give full disclosure of use of the AI product. For example, a physician using an expert system to diagnose a medical problem should get informed consent from the patient by stating (or having the patient sign in writing) that he or she is using an expert system.

Third, the AI developer should give notice/warnings to the user. For example, notices should be placed on the building in the robot work area to tell users of the "dos" and "don'ts" when working with or on the robots.

Fourth, the AI developer should do a legal search of copyrights, patents, and trademarks to see what others have done to protect themselves from infringing upon the rights of others and to accordingly protect his or her product from being copied by other developers/manufacturers.

Fifth, the AI developer should be aware of the use of run-time licenses, which for a set fee (or certain dollar amount per copy), an AI product can be sold to others by a buyer of that product. For example, if an expert system is being developed using an expert system shell and the user of the shell wants to sell his or her newly created expert system to others, then he or she normally needs to pay a run-time license to the expert system shell developer to do so.

Sixth, the AI developer should perform preventive maintenance (as well as corrective maintenance) on appropriate AI products, like robots. This will help ensure the proper working order of the robot and will limit the risk of accidents to the workers.

Finally, if there is a standard of care for computer use in a particular profession, then a person (i.e., the AI developer) should know clearly what is expected of him or her and act accordingly. Additionally, the AI developer should purchase professional liability/ malpractice insurance appropriate to his or her field [5].

The following are views on liability, according to Gemignani [8]:

Expert systems present novel issues concerning liability for injuries caused by their malfunction, particularly liability to third party clients and patients of system end users. Insofar as they are merely reference or consultative works, there is little chance that their designers and publishers will be found liable for malfunctions. If the expert system, however, becomes a more active participant in the decision-making process—in particular, if it gathers data itself, such as analyzing a patient's blood, or taking and interpreting a patient's EKG, then liability may follow if such data gathering itself is defective because the end user would have to rely on the accuracy of such system-produced data in interpreting the system's conclusions. The more directly the expert system affects the third party client or patient, the greater the chance the manufacturer will be liable, particularly if there is a direct contractual relationship with the end user and the foreseeability of harm to the third party if a malfunction occurs. As such systems improve, there is even the possibility that professionals will be held liable for failure to use them.

ORGANIZATIONAL CONSIDERATIONS IN DISTRIBUTING EXPERT SYSTEMS

When institutionalizing expert systems, the method for distributing the expert system and each new release must be carefully considered. For example, if it is to be distributed internally within an organization to 2,000 employees, then would it be best to make individual copies for each person's PC, or would it be better to put the expert system on a VAX, for example, and use dumb terminals for the employees to access the expert system? This question leads to several important points.

First, does the organization want to be in the business of making a tremendous number of copies of the expert system, particularly every time it is updated? This can be very burdensome and tedious, but perhaps one of the duties of an organization's information center might be to make copies of the expert system software, assuming proper legal authorization. It might be easier to put the system on a mainframe and let the employees access the expert system, through the network, to their terminal. One major question with this latter method is: How many users can concurrently access and use the expert system at any one time?

A second important point deals with the issue of run-time licenses. This topic was discussed previously in the chapter and there are certain license agreements that would need to be signed in order to make multiple copies. Some expert system vendors will let you pay one price and you can make as many multiple copies as you would like. Other vendors will let you pay a one-time price but you are restricted to making copies only within your organization. Still other expert system vendors will charge you per copy. When planning the design of the expert system, the issue of run-time licensing should be thought out in advance in order to ease the expert system institutionalization process.

A third point related to the initial question of distribution deals with security or tampering with the knowledge base. If everyone gets his or her own run-time version of the expert system, then there isn't much of a threat that the knowledge base will be tampered with. If the expert system is put on a mainframe and all people can gain access to the expert system, then the issue of tampering with the knowledge base has to be carefully considered.

The fourth point dealing with the initial distribution question has to do with two issues: maintenance and response time. Maintenance might be easier in using an expert system on the mainframe and then allowing people to gain access to it through their terminal. However, in terms of gaining access to the system and the response time in working through the session, the "single expert system concept" on the mainframe would probably be less favorable than the concept of each person having his or her own copy of the expert system on the PC. Maintaining the expert system for use on the PC is not cumbersome, but making multiple copies of the revised expert system, with each update, can be a great imposition.

Another important issue relating to distribution of expert systems is the need for an infrastructure in the organization that will support the user-oriented services associated with the new releases of the expert system. A group needs to be established within the company—perhaps through the information center or the expert system maintenance group—to update the documentation, provide training associated with the new features of the updated expert system, and provide other user support services associated with each new release of the expert system. Even though the expert system is maintained, if the users are not "retrained" on the new features of the expert system, then the institutionalization process of the expert system will falter. There not only has to be a group or individual to maintain the expert system, but also there must be the updating and retooling of the user's knowledge with each new release of the system.

CONCLUSIONS

The expert system institutionalization process encompasses important legal and organizational distribution issues that greatly affect the adoption of the expert system among the user community. Careful consideration must be given, in advance, to these issues. If these areas are recognized during the planning stages of the expert system's development, then there will be a greater likelihood for success when institutionalizing the expert system.

REFERENCES

[1]   Eliot, L.B., "Trends: The Commercialization of Expert Systems and Neural Networks," *IEEE Expert*, IEEE, Los Alamitos, CA, Summer 1988.

[2]   Hayes, C., "The Problems of Artificial Intelligence," *Palm Beach Review*, December 28, 1988, pp. 11–12.

[3]   Hyman, W.A., W.L. Johnston, and S. Spar, "Knowledge Based and Expert Systems: System Safety and Legal Issues in AI," *Computers & Industrial Engineering*, Pergamon Press, New York, Vol. 15, Nos. 1–4, 1988.

[4]   Zeide, J.S. and J. Liebowitz, "A Critical Review of Legal Issues in Artificial Intelligence," in *Managing AI and Expert Systems*, D.A. DeSalvo and J. Liebowitz (eds.), Prentice Hall, Englewood Cliffs, NJ, 1990.

[5]   Liebowitz, J. and J.S. Zeide, "A Little Legal Common Sense for AI Developers," *AI Week*, AI Week Inc., Birmingham, AL, January 15, 1989.

[6]   Frank, S.J., "What AI Practitioners Should Know About the Law: Part One," *AI Magazine*, American Association for Artificial Intelligence, Menlo Park, CA, Vol. 9, No. 1, 1988.

[7]   Frank, S.J., "What AI Practitioners Should Know About the Law: Part Two," *AI Magazine*, American Association for Artificial Intelligence, Menlo Park, CA, Vol. 9, No. 2, Summer 1988.

[8]   Gemignani, M.C., "Potential Liability for Use of Expert Systems," *IDEA-The Journal of Law and Technology*, 1989.

CHAPTER 10

SUMMARY OF EXPERT SYSTEM INSTITUTIONALIZATION GUIDELINES FOR ORGANIZATIONS

As discussed, many expert system projects fail due to poor transitioning or institutionalization. The issues of maintenance, distribution, implementation, training, and user support are too often overlooked in the expert systems life cycle process. These issues should be thought out and wrestled with far in advance during the planning stages of the expert system. Maintainability of the expert system is critical in achieving a good likelihood for success of the expert system among the users. A beautifully designed expert system may be useless unless it is properly maintained and updated. It is similar to having an accurate and complete knowledge base and efficient inference engine in the expert system, but a poor user interface. If the user has a hard time accessing the system, then it wouldn't be used. Bethlehem Steel learned this lesson the hard way by designing an expert system to help in the steel manufacturing process. Bethlehem Steel designed this expert system for the assembly line worker as the user, but even though the expert system was extremely accurate, the user interface was ill-designed because it required the workers to take off their gloves to use the keyboard. First of all, the line workers were not comfortable with computers and secondly, it was very awkward to be working on the line and then taking off and putting on the gloves to work the computer. The poorly designed user interface inhibited the use of the expert system—perhaps the user interface should have incorporated the use of light pens or touch screens. This expert system was never utilized because of this ill-designed user interface. In the same manner, if an expert system developer does not, up front, seriously think about the institutionalization process of the expert system, then the expert system will have a great chance of failure.

There have been many important lessons learned from implementing expert systems within organizations. The following are some learned in implementing expert systems for clinical trials data analyses [1]:

- Even though the technology is new, the old standards for building good systems still hold. For example, in selecting the development tools—both hardware and software—keep in mind the ultimate working environment in which the expert system must operate.
- The expert system itself will ultimately be only one part of the production system, albeit a key one. Building the other modules represents a significant additional expense in time and costs.
- The real world is full of messy details that must be resolved before the production system can be made operational. Dealing with them can double development time.
- Using new techniques such as expert systems can produce results that take on new and, perhaps, unconventional forms. This might require finding new ways to look at, interpret, and analyze the results.
- New ideas often feed upon themselves. Experimenting with expert systems will often suggest even more innovative ideas that can be investigated. If you live in a rigorous real-world production-oriented environment, you may need to resist this

trend and focus on the production work goal. If you are fortunate, you can pursue some of them and, perhaps, add to the body of knowledge.

This chapter summarizes the guidelines that the manager of an expert systems project should follow when institutionalizing expert systems. These guidelines are highlights from the previous chapters.

GUIDELINES FOR PROPER INSTITUTIONALIZATION OF EXPERT SYSTEMS

One of the most important points that a manager of an expert systems project should understand is to know the corporate culture in which the expert system will be deployed. Planning for the institutionalization process must be thought out well in advance, as early as the requirements analysis stage. The manager of the expert system project must anticipate the reactions of the intended users and must do everything possible in order to ensure a successful implementation of the expert system. The manager must understand the user community and their views of and comfortability in working with computers. The expert system manager must do everything in his or her power to ensure acceptance of the expert system among the users. Through user training, help desks, information centers, good documentation, and hotlines, the manager can provide mechanisms to reduce the pangs of the user in dealing with a "new" system or technology. By providing these services to the user, he or she may be less likely to resist change.

A corollary to this first guideline is the principle of soliciting and incorporating users' comments during the design, development, and implementation stages of the expert system. By getting users actively involved early on in the expert system life cycle development effort, they will feel that they are an important component of the expert system's development. Incorporating users' comments into each version of the expert system will give them a sense of commitment to and pride in the project. This will reduce barriers to implementing the expert system later on. Also, by integrating users' comments with the expert system during development, there will be a greater chance for strong user acceptance by the time the institutionalization process begins.

Another critical guideline for the expert system manager in properly institutionalizing the expert system within the organization is to make sure that there is a team/individual to maintain the expert system. Knowledge is forever expanding, and the expert system should constantly reflect this new knowledge as it pertains to the expert system's domain. A tax expert system may be useless if it reflects outdated tax laws, or a medical diagnosis expert system may not be consulted if it doesn't reflect the most recent medical findings pertinent to that expert system's domain. Placing an individual or team of persons whose duties include maintaining the expert system is a critical factor to promoting the use of the expert system. Of course, if the system is to be maintained and perhaps enhanced, then the users should be provided user training, appropriate user support services, and revised user documentation to accompany each new release of the updated expert system. Maintenance of the expert system must be considered during the planning stage of the expert system. The expert system manager must get the commitment from appropriate individuals who will be involved in maintaining the expert system.

For proper institutionalization of the expert system, the expert system manager must be very cognizant of the possible legal problems resulting from the use (and misuse) of the expert system. The issue of liability if the system gives incorrect advice and the issue of ownership are examples of legal areas which must be strongly considered by the manager when planning and developing the system. Possible legal problems must be anticipated by the manager and precautions must be taken to safeguard, as best as possible, against legal actions. The use of regulatory agencies, like the Food and Drug Administration which oversees medical expert systems, should help to ensure verification and validation of the expert system by setting strict standards. This will hopefully reduce the likelihood for lawsuits resulting from expert system use.

Another important guideline is to determine, during the planning stages, how the expert system will be distributed. The type of hardware platform is an important criterion when determining the design of the expert system. Some expert systems may be written in Lisp on the Lisp machine, and then deployed in C on the 386 PCs. If there will be several thousand users of the expert system, the manager must determine if it is better to make copies of the expert system and its updates for each user or should the expert system perhaps reside on a mainframe and then be downloaded to users. The questions of security, run-time licenses, site licenses, and making multiple copies of each new release need to be carefully considered by the expert system manager during the planning stages. These will later affect the institutionalization of the expert system.

The last major guideline is to keep the company's awareness of expert systems at a high level throughout the system's development and implementation, and even after its institutionalization. By building a well-validated, easy to use, expert system and by "well-institutionalizing" it, a positive image of expert systems will hopefully be created throughout the company. Even after this system is institutionalized, its manager should create and maintain a high awareness level of expert system technology among top management. In this manner, top management and others in the company will be well attuned to the concept and applications of expert systems. This may help in stimulating support for future expert system applications.

CONCLUSIONS

An expert system may be very accurate, but if it is not properly "institutionalized" within the organization, then it won't be utilized by the intended users. When planning and designing an expert system, careful and serious thought must be given to the institutionalization process. In the same manner, the design of the user interface must be thoughtfully determined during the beginning of the expert system life cycle process. The focus in designing the system is on the users' needs, and this focus carries over into its implementation and institutionalization. The manager of the expert systems project must make sure that the users' needs are addressed, and must provide the necessary user support services in order to ensure successful institutionalization.

REFERENCES

[1]   Long, J. M., J. R. Slagle, M. R. Wick, E. A. Irani, P. R. Weisman, J. P. Matts, P. F. Clarkson, and the POSCH Group, "Lessons Learned While Implementing Expert Systems in the Real World of Clinical Trials Data Analyses: The POSCH AI Project," *Proceedings* of International Workshop on Artificial Intelligence for Industrial Applications, IEEE, 1988.

In-Depth
Case Study
of CESA

CESA: AN EXPERT SYSTEM APPROACH TO HELPING THE CONTRACTING OFFICER TECHNICAL REPRESENTATIVE

INTRODUCTION

Expert systems are useful aids particularly in areas of "low interest, high utility." Contracting is one such area which, to a physicist, chemist, or computer scientist, may be of low interest but has high utility because each of these individuals will ultimately be involved in some form of contracting in order to perform his or her job, at least within the U.S. Government setting. At the Naval Research Laboratory, an expert system called CESA (COTR Expert System Aid)* has been developed to provide advice on pre-award areas in contracting. This case study will explain CESA's development process, testing and evaluation procedures, and institutionalization process.

*Developed at the U.S. Navy Center for Applied Research in Artificial Intelligence, Naval Research Laboratory, Washington, DC.

At the Naval Research Laboratory (NRL) a need was expressed by one of the scientists to possibly use expert systems technology to aid in the contracting process. This request came from a member of the Contracting Officer Technical Representative (COTR) community at the Laboratory. The COTR is an individual who ultimately monitors a contract once it has been awarded, and usually is the same person who assembles the procurement request package which leads to the contract award. The main difficulty in this process, in terms of the COTR's responsibilities, is the ability to put together a complete and accurate procurement request package. This pre-award area is somewhat arduous because there are a myriad of rules, regulations, and forms that the COTR needs to be familiar with in terms of contracting.

To help the COTR better perform his or her functions in the pre-award area, an expert system called CESA (COTR Expert System Aid) has been developed. CESA is, at present, a 210 rule-based expert system, developed using Exsys Professional, and runs on the IBM PC/AT.

CESA (COTR Expert System Aid) is an expert system field test prototype for helping the Acquisition Request Originator (ARO)/Contracting Officer Technical Representative (COTR) answer questions relating mostly to a contract's pre-award phase. CESA has been built at the U.S. Navy Center for Applied Research in Artificial Intelligence at the Naval Research Laboratory. CESA is designed to act as an advisory system to aid the ARO/COTR in assembling complete Procurement Request (PR) packages and in keeping up to date with the many changing regulations in Contracts that affect the ARO/COTR. The ARO is responsible for handling the pre-award phase of a potential contract, and after the contract is awarded, the COTR then is responsible for monitoring the contract. In all practicality, the ARO and the COTR are usually the same person at the Naval Research Laboratory.

With the myriad of Contracts' rules and regulations, it is very difficult for the typical ARO/COTR to stay abreast of these, especially since they also change often. Additionally, the ARO/COTR is not enthusiastically interested in the procurement process because the contracts procurement process is outside the main interest of the typical ARO/COTR. At the Naval Research Laboratory, the average

ARO/COTR is a physicist, chemist, mathematician, engineer, or computer scientist.

To help with the accuracy of advice in the procurement process and to make the procurement process a more enjoyable, less time-consuming process for the ARO/COTR, CESA was designed to help the ARO/COTR in the following major areas:

- To aid in answering questions relating to the pre-award phase of a contract.
- To aid in obtaining advice for completing selected pre-award forms and showing sample completions.
- To help in obtaining information about selected post-award areas.

In the following sections, the traditional expert system life cycle development steps [1,2,3,4] will be described as they pertain to CESA.

PROBLEM SELECTION

Upon receiving a request from one of the COTRs to look into expert systems for helping the COTR perform his or her responsibilities, the Navy Center for Applied Research in Artificial Intelligence undertook a three-month feasibility study to determine if, and where, expert systems would aid the COTR. In the feasibility study, four possible alternatives for expert system development were identified for aiding the COTR [5]—expert systems: for procurement request generation and routing; to act as a training aid; for specific problem-solving activities relating to the performance of a contract; and for monitoring the progress of a contract. Through analysis using the Analytic Hierarchy Process [5,6] and further discussions with COTRs and contracting specialists, the problem-solving alternative was ranked as the best choice.

After identifying our expert, who had over 26 years of experience in contracting, it was determined that the focus of the CESA prototype would be on the contracts pre-award area. The next step involved acquiring knowledge from the expert and from reading various documentation.

KNOWLEDGE ACQUISITION

Before beginning our interviews with the expert, the CESA knowledge engineering team enrolled in two courses: the ARO (Acquisition Request Originator) course and the COTR course. The ARO is technically the individual involved with the pre-award phase of a contract, and then the COTR takes over during the post-award phase once the contract is awarded. At the Naval Research Laboratory, however, the ARO and the COTR are usually the same individual. The courses provided the knowledge engineers with a good background on the concepts, terms, and range of activities that involve the COTR. Various booklets, such as the ARO Handbook and the COTR Handbook, as well as numerous NRL instructions, were read in order to better acquaint the knowledge engineering team with the problem domain.

After obtaining this preliminary background, the knowledge engineers met with the expert once a week for two hours for almost a year. Through interacting with the expert, the problem domain was scoped to include the following:

- Adequacy of the procurement request package.
  - What is needed in a PR package.
  - Justification and approval if requirement to be specified is sole source.
  - Evaluation.
  - Synopsis procedures.
  - The ADP Procurement Checklist.
- Routing of procurement documents.
- Use of the procurement planning document (PPD).
- Advice on how to complete selected pre-award forms.

Each knowledge acquisition session was structured to delve consecutively into each of these areas. After each knowledge acquisition session, the knowledge would be encoded into CESA that week and then CESA would be shown to the expert in the next session. This enabled the expert to provide feedback on the correctness and completeness of the knowledge in CESA. Also, it showed the expert that substantive results were being made after each knowledge engineering session. Once the knowledge was incrementally acquired, the next step involved representing the knowledge.

KNOWLEDGE REPRESENTATION

Since the expert talked in terms of SITUATION-ACTION clauses and because the contracting documentation actually were written in many IF-THEN expressions, it was decided that a rule-based format should be used for representing the knowledge in CESA. The first version of the CESA prototype had 146 rules. The second version of CESA has 210 rules. An example of one of CESA's rules is:

RULE NUMBER:56
IF: (1) Your questions involve the pre-award phase
      and (2) You need to explore adequacy of PR package items
      and (3) You want to know about what is needed in a PR
            package
      and (4) Your procurement is a major procurement costing
            $25,000 or more
      and (5) Procurement request is for capital equipment
THEN: Procurement Request for Purchase of Industrial Fund
      Equipment (NDW-NRL 4235/2431 (Rev 1-87))—YELLOW
      FORM-Confidence-10/10

The next step involved encoding the knowledge in CESA after it had been represented.

KNOWLEDGE ENCODING

To develop CESA in a timely fashion for prototyping purposes, it was decided that an expert system shell may be helpful in building CESA. The shell would have to fit the following requirements: run on an IBM PC or compatible; be easy to learn and maintain; allow for rule-based representation; include backward chaining (and possibly forward chaining) capabilities; be able to handle uncertainty; be affordable; have an affordable price for buying a run-time site license; allow links to external programs and databases; and provide a capability for the user to back up to previous questions in order to reenter a response. After reviewing the expert system shells available, it was decided that Exsys Professional would be appropriate and advisable for CESA's development. It should be noted that the 2.0 version of Exsys Professional handles hypertext—hypertext may be used later in CESA.

The process of encoding the knowledge was an iterative, rapid prototyping approach. Knowledge refinement and augmentation was conducted through the feedback and comments from the expert and users. Figure A-1 shows a sample annotated user session with CESA. After encoding the knowledge, the next step was to perform knowledge testing and evaluation.

TESTING AND EVALUATION OF CESA: PRELIMINARY EFFORTS

Since expert system building uses a rapid prototyping approach, testing was performed iteratively during each version of CESA. Testing, in this sense, refers to both verification and validation. During

```
CESA (COTR Expert System Aid)
```

```
    by:Jay Liebowitz, Laura Davis, and
       Wilson Harris
       EXPERT CONSULTANT: VIRGINIA DEAN


       Press any key to start:
```

Figure A-1, Screen 1   Annotated sample user session

Welcome to CESA--COTR Expert System Aid. This
expert system prototype will help you answer
questions pertinent to problems you might be
having as an ARO/COTR. To operate CESA,
respond to questions with the number of the
appropriate response and then press ENTER.
For multiple answers, put the number of the
answers and separate them with a comma (for
example 1,2). If you are not sure why a
question is being asked, then type the word
why. If you would like a description of the
terms used in the question, then type a
question mark (?). At the end of your session,
the conclusions will be displayed ranked in
importance by a value from 1 (least often
applies) to 10 (most often applies). Happy
contracting!

                Press any key to start:

Figure A-1, Screen 2

Your questions involve the
        1   pre-award phase
        2   post-award phase
1

* Remember to type in the number of the
  appropriate response and then press ENTER. *

Enter the number of ONLY ONE value   WHY to
display rule being used
<?> for details   QUIT to save data   <H>
for help   <Ctrl-U> to undo

Figure A-1, Screen 3

You have specific preaward questions on
    1   adequacy of the procurement request
        (PR) package
    2   routing of procurement documents
    3   use of the procurement planning
        document (PPD)
    4   advice on how to complete selected
        pre-award forms
1

* If you want to "back up" to up to 10
previous questions (i.e., you might have made
a mistake), then press the "CTRL" key and the
"u" key (hold the CTRL key while you press the
u key). *

Enter the number of ONLY ONE value   WHY to
display rule being used
<?> for details   QUIT to save data   <H>
for help   <Ctrl-U> to undo

Figure A-1, Screen 4

You want to know about
    1 what is needed in a PR package
    2 Justification and Approval (J&A) if
      requirement to be specified is sole
      source
    3 evaluation
    4 synopsis procedures
    5 the ADP Procurement Checklist
1

Enter the number of ONLY ONE value   WHY to
display rule being used
<?> for details   QUIT to save data   <H>
for help   <Ctrl-U> to undo

Figure A-1, Screen 5

Your procurement is a
       1 major procurement costing $25,000 or
          more
       2 procurement under $25,000
1

Enter the number of ONLY ONE value   WHY to
display rule being used
<?> for details   QUIT to save data   <H>
for help   <Ctrl-U> to undo

Figure A-1, Screen 6

Contract
       1 involves access to, receipt of, or
          generation of classified material and/
          or access to classified areas
       2 does NOT involve access to, receipt
          of, or generation of classified
          material and/or access to classified
          areas
1

Enter the number of ONLY ONE value   WHY to
display rule being used
<?> for details   QUIT to save data   <H>
for help   <Ctrl-U> to undo

Figure A-1, Screen 7

Your procurement is
    1   competitive
    2   sole source (noncompetitive)
    3   for an 8a small disadvantaged business
    4   a Broad Agency Announcement (BAA)
        response (assume BAA for unsolicited
        UNIVERSITY proposals)
?

* You can type in a ? if you want a better
description of the question. If no
descriptions are provided when you type ?,
then the statement "No explanation available"
will be shown on the screen. *

Enter the number of ONLY ONE value   WHY to
display rule being used
<?> for details   QUIT to save data   <H>
for help   <Ctrl-U>   to undo

Figure A-1, Screen 8

An 8a small disadvantaged business is a Small
Business Administration certified "small
business concern owned and controlled by
socially and economically disadvantaged
individuals." See ARO Handbook for further
guidance. Most unsolicited proposals relate
to elements of published BAAs. Advantages to
treating your procurement as a response to a
BAA include elimination of synopsis and J&A
requirements. Contact your Contracts Support
Code for further BAA information.

TO RETURN TO PROGRAM PRESS <SPACE>

* To have the question reasked after typing ?,
press the space bar. *

Figure A-1, Screen 9

Your procurement is
    1 competitive
    2 sole source (noncompetitive)
    3 for an 8a small disadvantaged business
    4 a Broad Agency Announcement (BAA)
      response (assume BAA for unsolicited
      UNIVERSITY proposals)
1

Enter the number of ONLY ONE value   WHY to
display rule being used
<?> for details   QUIT to save data   <H>
for help   <Ctrl-U> to undo

Figure A-1, Screen 10

Procurement request is for
    1 capital equipment
    2 sponsor-funded equipment
    3 neither capital equipment nor
      sponsor-funded equipment
why

* If you want to see the rule which is being
worked on, then type "why". *

Enter the number of ONLY ONE value   WHY to
display rule being used
<?> for details   QUIT to save data   <H>
for help   <Ctrl-U> to undo

Figure A-1, Screen 11

RULE NUMBER: 56
IF:

      (1)   Your questions involve the pre-award
           phase
and   (2)   You need to explore adequacy of PR
           package items
and   (3)   You want to know about what is
           needed in a PR package
and   (4)   Your procurement is a major
           procurement costing $25,000 or more
and   (5)   Procurement request is for capital
           equipment

THEN:

         Procurement Request for Purchase of
         Industrial Fund Equipment (NDW-NRL
         4235/2431 (Rev 1-87)--YELLOW
         FORM-Confidence=10/10

REFERENCE: NRLINST 4205.3A (April 19, 1988)

* To see the reference of the rule, type "r". *

Press any key to continue:

Figure A-1, Screen 12

Procurement request is for
       1 capital equipment
       2 sponsor-funded equipment
       3 neither capital equipment nor
          sponsor-funded equipment
3

Enter the number of ONLY ONE value   WHY to
display rule being used
<?> for details   QUIT to save data   <H>
for help   <Ctrl-U> to undo

Figure A-1, Screen 13

Your procurement request deals with
    1 acquisition of commercially available
       hardware/software, services/
       maintenance, or materials where the
       vendor can quote a price that won't
       change during the life of the contract
       and can deliver at that price (vendor
       assumes risk)
    2 minor modification to hardware/
       software to suit government needs
       (vendor assumes risk)
    3 major R&D modification to
       hardware/software to suit government
       needs (government assumes risk)
    4 research and development of
       hardware/software (government assumes
       risk)
    5 R&D studies/services where NRL cannot
       define explicitly the requirements but
       can provide general work statements
       (government assumes risk)
    6 university research and development
       (government assumes risk)
    7 R&D acquisition (e.g., design and
       fabrication) of hardware/software with
       explicit specifications (vendor
       assumes risk)
5

Enter the number of ONLY ONE value   WHY to
display rule being used
<?> for details   QUIT to save data   <H>
for help   <Ctrl-U> to undo

Figure A-1, Screen 14

PR involves a(n)
     1 new research effort at NRL
     2 existing research effort at NRL
1

Enter the number of ONLY ONE value   WHY to
display rule being used
<?> for details   QUIT to save data   <H>
for help   <Ctrl-U> to undo

Figure A-1, Screen 15

Your procurement involves
     1 nonpersonal services (e.g., research
        study, maintenance)
     2 personal services (e.g., data entry,
        secretarial)
     3 products rather than services (e.g.,
        hardware, software)
1

Enter the number of ONLY ONE value   WHY to
display rule being used
<?> for details   QUIT to save data   <H>
for help   <Ctrl-U> to undo

Figure A-1, Screen 16

```
acquired services are
     1  being funded with RDT&E (research,
        development, testing and evaluation)
        dollars
     2  NOT being funded with RDT&E dollars
1
```

```
Enter the number of ONLY ONE value   WHY to
display rule being used
<?>  for details    QUIT to save data    <H>
for help    <Ctrl-U>  to undo
```

Figure A-1, Screen 17

```
contract is (PLEASE HIT ? FOR DESCRIPTION OF
ADP BEFORE ENTERING YOUR RESPONSE)
     1  ADP (Automatic Data Processing)
     2  non-ADP
?
```

```
Enter the number of ONLY ONE value   WHY to
display rule being used
<?>  for details    QUIT to save data    <H>
for help    <Ctrl-U>  to undo
```

Figure A-1, Screen 18

ADP typically includes computers, ancillary
equipment, software, firmware, services, and
related resources as defined by regulations
issued by GSA. ADP does NOT include ADP
equipment acquired by a federal contractor
which is incidental to the performance of a
federal contract; radar, sonar, radio, or TV
equipment; or procurement by DOD of ADP
equipment or services for intelligence
operations.

TO RETURN TO PROGRAM PRESS <SPACE>

Figure A-1, Screen 19

contract is (PLEASE HIT ? FOR DESCRIPTION OF
ADP BEFORE ENTERING YOUR RESPONSE)
     1 ADP (Automatic Data Processing)
     2 non-ADP
1

Enter the number of ONLY ONE value   WHY to
display rule being used
<?> for details   QUIT to save data   <H>
for help   <Ctrl-U> to undo

Figure A-1, Screen 20

PR involves a new contract or a modification
to the contract
        1 in excess of $100,000
        2 NOT in excess of $100,000
1

Enter the number of ONLY ONE value   WHY to
display rule being used
<?> for details   QUIT to save data   <H>
for help   <Ctrl-U> to undo

Figure A-1, Screen 21

Company/product/service relating to the PR is
        1 on the GSA schedule
        2 NOT on the GSA schedule
1

Enter the number of ONLY ONE value   WHY to
display rule being used
<?> for details   QUIT to save data   <H>
for help   <Ctrl-U> to undo

Figure A-1, Screen 22

Product relating to the PR is
     1 competitive on the GSA schedule (i.e.,
        product or similar item available from
        at least two offerors on the GSA
        schedule)
     2 NOT competitive on the GSA schedule
1

Enter the number of ONLY ONE value   WHY to
display rule being used
<?> for details   QUIT to save data   <H>
for help   <Ctrl-U> to undo

Figure A-1, Screen 23

Thank you for using CESA. Please hit any key
to display the conclusions.

* Remember to do this! *

Press any key to display results:

Figure A-1, Screen 24

* Items 1 to 15 show you the conclusions based
upon your input. *

            Values based on 0-10 system   VALUE

1 Security Checklist; DD Form 254 (Rev
   1-78)--DOD Contract Security
   Classification Spec and Attachments;
   SCI Contract Support Information Sheet
   (NIC Form 5540/1 (Rev 10-85); NDW-NRL
   4200/1209 (9-86)--Procurement
   Request/Contract Information Sheet   10
2 Procurement Request (NDW-NRL 4235/2404
   (Rev 8-86)--WHITE FORM   10
3 Statement of Work (SOW)   10
4 NDW-NRL 3900/1002 (Rev 11-84)--Work
   Unit Assignment Summary (DD Form
   1498), required by Code 1005   10
5 ADP Approval Checklist with supporting
   documentation, and ADP System
   Accreditation Report, if purchasing or
   leasing ADP equipment or services   10
6 NDW-NRL 4205/1303 (5-87)--Format for
   Additional Resources Required for New
   and Existing Contracts   10
7 Evaluation criteria and weights;
   Evaluation plan, including list of
   recommended evaluation panel members   10
8 NPSQ (Nonpersonal Services
   Questionnaire)   10
9 Proposal Requirements documentation
   for inclusion in the

Press any key for more:

Figure A-1, Screen 25

Request for Proposals (RFP)   10
10 Contract Data Requirements List (Form
    DD1423)   10
11 Complete the MENS (Mission Element
    Needs) form.   10
12 Provide a source list of competitive
    bidders.   10
13 You need a 15-day intent synopsis.   10
14 You do NOT need NDW-NRL 4200/1293
    (2-86)--Contractor Advisory Assistant
    Services (CAAS) documentation   9
15 Appropriate type of contract is
    cost-plus-fixed-fee (CPFF) AND normally
    level-of-effort CPFF since Government is
    buying hours of effort resulting in
    research reports

All Choices <A>   only if value<1 <G>   Print
<P>   Change and rerun <C>
Rules used <line #>   Quit/save <Q>   Help
<H>   Done <D>:

Figure A-1, Screen 26

```
          Request for Proposals (RFP)              10
    10    Contract Data Requirements List (Form
          DD1423)                                  10
    11    Complete the MENS (Mission Element
          Needs) form,                             10
    12    Provide a source list of competitive
          bidders,                                 10
    13    You need a 15-day intent synopsis,       10
    14    You do NOT need NDW-NRL 4200/1293
          (2-86)--Contractor Advisory Assistant
          Services (CAAS) documentation             9
    15    Appropriate type of contract is
          cost-plus-fixed-fee (CPFF) AND normally
          level-of-effort CPFF since government is
          buying hours of effort resulting in
          research reports
```

* If you want to see all the conclusions
displayed, type A, *

* If you want to see why a conclusion was
reached, then type in the number associated
with that conclusion, The rule(s) will be
shown that triggered that conclusion, *

* Type P to get a printout of the knowledge
base, *

* Use shift-Prtsc to get a printout of your
conclusions screens *

* Typing C allows you to see your input and
to quickly make changes, *

```
All Choices <A>    only if value>1 <G>    Print
<P>    Change and rerun <C>
Rules used <line #>   Quit/save <Q>    Help
<H>    Done <D>:   10
```

Figure A-1, Screen 27

RULE NUMBER: 83   RULE TRUE
IF:

    (1) Your questions involve the preaward
          phase
and (2) need to explore adequacy of PR
          package items
and (3) You want to know about what is needed
          in a PR package
and (4) Your procurement is a major
          procurement costing \$25,000 or more
and (5) Appropriate type of contract is
          cost-plus-fixed-fee (CPFF) OR
          cost-reimbursement (CR)

THEN:

       Contract Data Requirements List
       (Form DD1423) - Confidence=10/10

* To end a session, type ''d'' for DONE. *

* When CESA asks you to run (Y/N), type n for
no or y for yes. *

If line # for derivation, <K>-Known data,
<C>-choices, <R>-reference,
or - prev. or next rule, <J>-jump, <H>-help
or <ENTER> to continue:

Figure A-1, Screen 28

the demonstration prototype and research prototype versions of CESA, verification was performed by exhaustively checking all the possible combinations of responses in CESA in order to make sure that CESA was logically consistent and to be certain that all possible combinations of input were covered in CESA. Verification in this regard was a very time-consuming process. In the demonstration prototype version of CESA, there were 146 rules with the average rule containing about six antecedents and two consequents. The field test prototype version of CESA has 210 rules.

Validation was performed in various ways during CESA's development. First, backcasting was used in order to run CESA against historical test cases in order to compare CESA's results with the actual, documented results. In this regard, we ran CESA against actual PR files in order to compare results. We used 20 historical test cases, which consisted of "hard," "soft," and "special" cases. Hard cases are those classical test cases that fall squarely within the scope of CESA. Soft cases are those test cases that push the "boundary" of CESA in order to see the point at which CESA would degrade. Special cases are those used in order to determine the various exceptions to CESA's rules. As one might imagine in the contracts legal environment, there are many exceptions and even exceptions to the exceptions. These test cases were critical to ensuring the quality of advice in CESA. Nazareth [7], Harrison [8], Jacobs et al. [9], and Liebowitz [10] provide detailed considerations for testing and evaluation of expert systems.

We also used another expert in Contracts to run through sample scenarios using CESA and then critique CESA's results. Some areas surfaced that were overlooked and these comments were incorporated into CESA. A preliminary evaluation was also conducted by having various COTRs use CESA to comment on the human factors features in CESA. Questions had to be reworded, free-text comments describing various definitions had to be included, and the presentation of conclusions had to be reworked. Specifically, the users liked the ability in CESA to back up to 10 previous questions in a user session in order to reenter a new response or correct a response. A more extensive testing and evaluation plan was exercised in the field test prototype version of CESA. This will be explained next.

TESTING AND EVALUATION OF CESA: METHODS

After incorporating the comments of the experts and other users into CESA, we felt confident that we had a field test prototype version of CESA that could then be more formally evaluated. To accomplish this testing and evaluation, we selected a test group of four individuals, based on the following guidelines:

1. Level of user knowledge:
   1 user: experienced user (e.g., Facilities Manager).
   2 users: naive users (one with zero to one year of ARO experience; the other with two to four years).
   1 user: knowledgeable user (five to eight years of ARO experience).

2. Affiliation within NRL: The users should be selected from among the directorates at NRL. It would be useful to have users from directorates that are having problems in putting together PR packages and/or are inundated with a large volume of PR packages that need to be assembled. Also, the user sample, as a whole, should represent the variety of PR actions that can result in the laboratory.

3. Willingness to be a CESA user: The most important characteristic in selecting a user for the CESA test and evaluation team is the willingness of the user to participate in this project. It is undesirable to have a user participate in this project only because his or her superior mandates this request. The user will need to spend about 20 to 25 hours in one calendar month as part of the test and evaluation phase for the CESA prototype. This time will be devoted to training on how to work CESA, letting the user during the month obtain hands-on experience in running numerous sample runs with CESA, answering evaluation questionnaires on various aspects of CESA, and meeting and interacting with the CESA development team.

4. Hardware: The user must have access to an IBM PC or PC compatible.

5. Follow-up work based on the T&E results: User feedback during

the T&E stage of CESA will be incorporated into the following version of CESA. With the inclusion of these comments in CESA, CESA will then be field tested to a larger group of users at NRL.

The test group was then selected based upon these guidelines.

The first meeting with the test group served as an introduction to CESA and we laid out the testing and evaluation plans for the coming month. Each participant received a folder which included: (1) Quick reference user documentation using CESA via Exsys Professional, including an annotated sample user session of CESA, (2) testing and evaluation schedule, (3) 11 evaluation questionnaires, and (4) disks for using CESA. At the meeting, we presented an overview on CESA and its development and then presented the testing and evaluation schedule and evaluation questionnaires. Figure A-2 shows the testing and evaluation schedule and Figures A-3–5 present three of the evaluation questionnaires. After discussing the upcoming plans for testing and evaluation, we gathered around the computer and ran through a sample session of CESA using an example from one of the participants. The useful features of CESA were pointed out during the user session. Some of these included:

- Typing "why" to see the rule that CESA is working on.
- Typing "?" to see a free-text comment for a definition or description of a term.
- Typing "CTRL-U" to back up to a previous question to input a new response.
- Typing "C" for change and rerun in order to quickly see the inputs provided during the sample run, and then quickly being able to change your input and rerun.
- Typing "P" to get a printout of the input and results.

After the CESA demonstration, the participants embarked on their schedules to use CESA each week and turn in the appropriate evaluation questionnaires due at the end of each week.

May 23   Training Session

May 24–31   ● Use CESA to run at least five historical test cases in
              "What's needed in PR package"

            ● Try out areas (under adequacy of PR package)
              —"Evaluation"
              —"Synopsis"
              —"Justification & Approval if requirement to be
              specified is sole source"

June 1   Submit to Jay Liebowitz, Code 5510:
              ● Printout of input and output for historical test cases
              ● Evaluation forms #1, 2, 3, 4

June 1–8   ● Use CESA to run at least five new test cases in
              "What's needed in PR package"

            ● Try out areas
              —Use of ADP Procurement Checklist
              —Routing of Procurement Documents
              —Use of the Procurement Planning Document

June 8   Submit to Jay Liebowitz, Code 5510
              ● Printout of input and output for new test cases
              ● Evaluation forms #5, 6, 7, 8

June 8–14   ● Use CESA to try out
              —Advice on Completing Pre-Award Forms
              —Post-Award Sections

June 15   Submit to Jay Leibowitz, Code 5510
              ● Evaluation Forms #9, 10, 11

June 22   9:00 am; Everyone gets together at AI Center for final
              testing and evaluation comments

Figure A-2   Testing and evaluation schedule for CESA

1. On a scale of 1 (lowest) to 10 (highest), what would you rate the usefulness of the "What's needed in a PR package" section? _____

2. How many historical test cases did you use in comparing CESA's results with the documented cases, in regards to "What's needed in a PR package?" _____

3. Please describe the discrepancies, if any, between CESA's results and the historical files in determining what forms were needed in a PR package:

   Test Case 1:   Discrepancies: Yes _____   No _____
   Explain discrepancies:

   Test Case 2:   Discrepancies: Yes _____   No _____
   Explain discrepancies:

   Test Case 3:   Discrepancies: Yes _____   No _____
   Explain discrepancies:

   Test Case 4:   Discrepancies: Yes _____   No _____
   Explain discrepancies:

   Test Case 5:   Discrepancies: Yes _____   No _____
   Explain discrepancies:

Figure A-3   Evaluation questionnaire 1
what's needed in a PR package—historical cases

4. Were there any questions or comments in using CESA that you did not understand? Explain.

5. In this section, please indicate improvements that you would like to see.

Figure A-3   (continued)

1. On a scale of 1 (lowest) to 10 (highest), what would you rate the usefulness of the "synopsis" section? _____

2. Please describe any discrepancies between CESA's results and what you feel is correct.

3. Were there any questions or comments in using CESA that you did not understand, in regards to the "synopsis section"? Explain.

4. Please indicate improvements that you would like to see in this section.

Figure A-4   Evaluation questionnaire 3
"adequacy of a PR package—synopsis"

To aid us in enhancing CESA, we kindly ask for your comments in completing this questionnaire. Please answer each question along the scale of 1 (lowest rating) to 10 (best rating), where appropriate. Your comments will be incorporated into the next version of CESA.

I. Quality of the Advice/Conclusions Reached

    a. After running CESA against historical cases in your files, how accurate were CESA's results?
       1 2 3 4 5 6 7 8 9 10

    b. How many historical test cases did you use? _____

    c. What discrepancies existed between CESA's results and your test files (please be specific)? _____

       _____

       _____

       _____

       _____

    d. When you used CESA for new test cases, how accurate were CESA's results?
       1 2 3 4 5 6 7 8 9 10

    e. How many new test cases did you use? _____

    f. What discrepancies existed between CESA's results and the results that you feel should be concluded for your new test cases? _____

       _____

       _____

       _____

II. Line of Questioning

    a. How would you rate the line of questioning that CESA used in terms of the logical and natural sequence of questions that you would ask to arrive at a conclusion?
       1 2 3 4 5 6 7 8 9 10

    b. What specifically should be changed, if any, regarding the ordering of the questions? _____

       _____

       _____

Figure A-5   Evaluation questionnaire 9

   c. Are there ways in which you would like to see a different approach to arriving at a conclusion? _____

_____

_____

   d. How helpful did you find the CTRL-U feature to back up to a previous question for re-entering your response?
1 2 3 4 5 6 7 8 9 10

III. Helpful Design Features (Discourse—Input/Output)

  A. Clarity and Completeness of Questions and Free-Text Comments

    a. How understandable were the questions that were being asked?
1 2 3 4 5 6 7 8 9 10

    b. How understandable were the definitions/descriptions when you typed a ? to a question?
1 2 3 4 5 6 7 8 9 10

    c. How complete were the definitions/descriptions in CESA?
1 2 3 4 5 6 7 8 9 10

    d. What suggestions can you make in order to improve the understandability and completeness of the questions and definitions/descriptions in CESA?

_____

_____

_____

_____

  B. Conclusions of CESA

    e. How helpful were the conclusions to you?
1 2 3 4 5 6 7 8 9 10

    f. How would you rate the presentation of conclusions as displayed on the screen?
1 2 3 4 5 6 7 8 9 10

Figure A-5 (continued)

g. What suggestions, if any, do you have regarding improving the ordering and presentation of conclusions?

_____

_____

_____

C. Explanations and Instructions

h. How helpful were the explanations to you when you typed "why" to a given question?
1   2   3   4   5   6   7   8   9   10

i. How clear and complete were the instructions given in CESA on how to work CESA?
1   2   3   4   5   6   7   8   9   10

j. What suggestions, if any, do you have regarding improving the explanations and instructions in CESA?

_____

_____

_____

D. Response Time and Hardware

k. How quick was CESA's response time in moving on to the next question?
1   2   3   4   5   6   7   8   9   10

l. How quick was the time needed to run through a full session of CESA?
1   2   3   4   5   6   7   8   9   10

m. How easy was it to learn how to work CESA?
1   2   3   4   5   6   7   8   9   10

n. How widely available is an IBM PC or PC-compatible in your colleagues' work area?
1   2   3   4   5   6   7   8   9   10

o. Would you prefer another type of computer to work CESA, like the Mac?   Yes _____   No _____

E. Graphics

p. How acceptable to you was the user interface in using CESA?
1   2   3   4   5   6   7   8   9   10

Figure A-5   (continued)

q. How great a need is there to use more graphics (i.e., pictures) in CESA?
1 2 3 4 5 6 7 8 9 10

r. What type of graphics capabilities, if any, would you like to see in CESA in order to make CESA easier to use?

_____

_____

_____

_____

IV. Utility

a. How many minutes/hours would it typically take you to determine what forms are needed to make up a PR package, without using CESA? _____

b. How many minutes did it take for you to run through a session of CESA to determine what's needed to make up your PR package? _____

c. Do you feel that there is a need for CESA among NRL's ARO/COTRs?
1 2 3 4 5 6 7 8 9 10

d. How pleased were you overall in CESA as an aid to help you with your pre-award questions?
1 2 3 4 5 6 7 8 9 10

e. What causes you the most trouble as a ARO/COTR? _____

_____

_____

_____

f. How useful do you find CESA as a training tool to supplement the ARO/COTR courses?
1 2 3 4 5 6 7 8 9 10

g. How useful do you find CESA as a tool to use in the actual operations of the everyday COTR?
1 2 3 4 5 6 7 8 9 10

h. Which area within CESA did you find the most helpful and the least helpful (rank in order of priority with 1 (least helpful) through 10 (most helpful)):

Figure A-5   (continued)

_____ what's needed in PR package
_____ J&A if requirement to be specified is sole source
_____ evaluation
_____ synopsis procedures
_____ use of ADP Procurement Checklist
_____ routing of procurement documents
_____ use of the PPD
_____ advice on how to complete selected pre-award forms

  i. What other pre-award areas would you like included in CESA?

_____

_____

_____

V. Future Work

  a. What improvements or enhancements would you like to see us incorporate into CESA, IN ORDER OF PRIORITY:

    1. _____

    2. _____

    3. _____

    4. _____

  b. How important is it to include actual PR forms in CESA?
    1 2 3 4 5 6 7 8 9 10

  c. How important is it to include in CESA advice for completing PR forms?
    1 2 3 4 5 6 7 8 9 10

  d. How important is it to include post-award information in CESA?
    1 2 3 4 5 6 7 8 9 10

  e. If CESA were released lab-wide, would you use CESA:
    _____ yes   _____ no
    How often would you use CESA?   _____ times per week

  f. How would you use CESA (please rank IN ORDER OF PRIORITY):
    _____ training new people
    _____ double-check your knowledge
    _____ help you in unfamiliar areas
    _____ other (please specify)

Figure A-5   (continued)

g. Please provide any other comments regarding CESA:

_____

_____

_____

Figure A-5   (continued)

TESTING AND EVALUATION OF CESA: RESULTS

The testing participants were fairly conscientious in working through sample sessions with CESA and completing each evaluation questionnaire on a timely basis. One of the participants, however, dropped out after the first week because of an unforeseen added workload in his normal duties. The specific comments and overall CESA evaluation results are shown in Figures A-6 and A-7.

What's Needed in PR Package:

- Need to handle modification to SOW (just need Additional Resources Form and mod to SOW; don't need to start as new package).
- Under $25K, need SOW and CDRL for study contract (maybe Patent Rights form).
- Add "student" contracts and change orders to existing contracts
- Give latest version of forms/instructions (e.g., NPSQ)
- Indicate whether synopsis is mandatory or recommended

Evaluation:

- Need examples.

Synopsis:

- Need cost reimbursement synposis shell.
- Indicate if synopsis is mandatory or recommended.

Figure A-6   Compilation of evaluation results

J&A if Requirement to be Specified is Sole Source:

● Indicate guidelines as to whether Acquisition Plan is applicable.
● Include more information about the signature page of J&A.

Use of ADP Procurement Checklist:

● States "Noncompetitive acquisition of ADP resources is prohibited"—does this mean no sole source ADP?
● Need more detailed instruction as to what goes into ADP checklist.
● Need to indicate the main points that the approving officials are looking for.

Routing of Procurement Documents:

● Need to indicate the internal routing of documents within Codes.
● Need more detailed routing.
● Need to state the review gates to Code 3202.

Use of the PPD:

● Explain specifically the contents of each package and the routing procedure within Codes.
● Give codes instead of "review gates."

Advice on Completing Sample Pre-Award Forms:

● The phrase, "The following advice should be used . . ." is redundant in the Justification for Other than Full and Open Competition—remove it.
● Make note at the end of the J&A instructions that this item should be on letterhead paper and should be signed by the COTR.

Post-Award Sections:

● Fill in missing post-award sections.

Figure A-6   (continued)

(Note: Scores range from 1 (lowest) to 10 (highest); Some testing participants did not indicate a score on all sections)

1. Quality of Advice/Conclusions Reached:

    9/10—the 45 day synopsis is optional and don't provide copies of the Work Units.
    9/10
    10/10

2. Line of Questioning: 10/10
    10/10

3. Understandability:

    a. Questions: 10/10
        10/10

    b. Definitions with ? mark: 8/10
        6/10

    c. Instructions: 10/10
        10/10

4. Completeness:

    a. Definitions with ? mark: 9/10
        10/10

    b. Instructions: 10/10
        10/10

5. Conclusions of CESA:

    a. Helpfulness: 10/10
        10/10

    b. Presentation of Conclusions: 10/10
        10/10

6. Response Time and Hardware:

    a. Quickness of response time in moving on to next question:
        10/10
        10/10

    b. Time needed to run through a full session: 10/10

    c. How easy to learn how to work CESA: 10/10
        10/10

Figure A-7   Overall evaluation of CESA

d. Preference to Hardware: 1—PC
                                    2—Mac
                                    3—another type of computer

7. Graphics:

   a. Acceptability of user interface: 10/10
                                           10/10
                                           4/10

8. Utility:

   a. How long before CESA: 10 minutes
                              30–45 min.
                              not long
      Using CESA: 5 min or less
                   5 min or less
                   quick and easy

   b. Need for CESA: 10/10
                       10/10
                       8/10

   c. Pleased overall with CESA: 10/10
                               10/10
                               8/10

   d. What causes you the most trouble as COTR:
   —preparing J&As
   —preparing Statements of Work and J&As
   —exact wording needed on forms

   e. CESA as training tool to supplement COTR courses: 8/10
                                                       8/10
                                                  10/10

   f. CESA as operational tool: 10/10
                             10/10
                             7/10

   g. Three most helpful areas in CESA:
   1. J&A if req to be specified is sole source
   2. what's needed in PR package
   3. advice on how to complete selected pre-award forms
   1. what's needed in PR package
   2. J&A if req to be specified is sole source
   3. use of ADP Procurement Checklist

      1. what's needed in PR package
      2. advice on how to complete selected pre-award forms
      3. J&A if req to be specified is sole source

   h. Three least helpful areas in CESA:
      1. routing of procurement documents
      2. use of the PPD
      3. evaluation
      1. evaluation
      2. routing of procurement documents
      3. use of PPD
      1. routing of procurement documents
      2. use of ADP Procurement Checklist
      3. synopsis procedures

9. Future Work:
   a. How important to include actual PR forms in CESA: 10/10
                                            2/10
                                          10/10

   b. How important to include advice on completing PR
     forms: 10/10
           10/10
           10/10 (include personal vs. nonpersonal information)

   c. How important to include post-award information: 10/10
                                          6/10
                                      10/10

   d. If CESA released lab-wide:
      1. Would you use CESA: Yes
                    Yes
                    Yes

      2. How often: 2–3 times per week
                5 times per week
                For each major contract

   e. Major benefit of CESA: Training new people
                          Training new people
                          Double-check your knowledge

Figure A-7   (continued)

Generally speaking, the users were very pleased with the accuracy of advice provided by CESA. The users were also impressed with the ease of use in working CESA. The test group felt that CESA would save them a lot of time in preparing procurement request packages which ultimately will speed up the time required to award their contracts. They felt that the major benefits of using CESA are training new people and double-checking the COTR's knowledge.

The test participants were very helpful in providing ways to correct and enhance CESA. They specifically wanted certain sections to be more comprehensive, for example, to indicate the specific codes for routing a procurement package instead of simply saying "route through the review gates." The test users suggested changes in the wording of questions, descriptions, and conclusions. There were other suggestions made regarding improving the usefulness of some sections in CESA. For example, the synopsis section should clearly indicate if the COTR has to prepare the synopsis or whether it is highly recommended that the COTR submit a draft of the synopsis.

As shown in Figure A-7, the overall evaluation of CESA was very positive and favorable. The understandability of the questions, advice, and instructions was high, and the completeness, helpfulness, and presentation of conclusions were rated highly. The users indicated that they would use CESA in their daily work and that the need for such a system was fully warranted.

OBSERVATIONS FROM THE TESTING AND EVALUATION EXERCISE

We, as the knowledge engineering team, noted some interesting observations during the testing and evaluation period. Some of these insights might help others when testing and evaluating their expert system.

One fascinating experience occurred at the beginning of the testing and evaluation period. This experience involved our domain expert. We were very fortunate to have worked with our domain expert, who had over 26 years of experience in contracting. She was very intelligent, articulate, cooperative, and focused. In fact, she was so excited about CESA that she felt that it was "her baby." This involvement and attachment is what we had wanted to achieve, in essence, being a project champion. In fact, her commitment and enthusiasm over CESA were so strong in that it caused some awkwardness during some of the testing and evaluation of CESA. At the beginning, when suggestions were made on how to correct and improve CESA, the expert took some of these comments personally. The expert felt that her knowledge was represented in the expert system, and her "domain" was being threatened somewhat when suggestions were being made as to what might be incorrect in CESA or what areas were omitted and should be included in CESA. To overcome this potential problem, the knowledge engineering team used written evaluation questionnaires which the test group would complete concerning each area in CESA. The written evaluations were then reviewed by the knowledge engineers and the expert. By having the testing and evaluation comments in writing, this created a less threatening situation for the expert instead of having face-to-face discussions and potential confrontations between the expert and test group.

A second observation concerns the testing and evaluation procedure in that this process should be fairly structured for the test group. To ensure that each test participant would try out each area within CESA, we used evaluation questionnaires that had to be completed by each participant on each part of CESA's knowledge base. The questionnaires forced each participant to review every part of CESA, instead of giving him or her free reign to choose which part of CESA to focus on or exclude. The questionnaires imposed some structure, but not enough to hinder creativity. Most of the questions were open-ended, so that participants could express exactly what they wanted.

A third observation concerns the length and format of the evaluation questionnaire. We purposefully made almost all of the questionnaires one to two pages in length, with about five or six questions. To ensure completion, we thought that we would have a better success rate with shorter forms. Also, we tried to standardize the questionnaire to make it easier for the participant to complete. By doing so, the participant was able to get into a framework and then anticipate what questions would be asked in evaluating later parts of CESA.

FUTURE TESTING AND EVALUATION

After taking three weeks to incorporate the suggestions from the initial testing group into CESA, the next step was fielding CESA to about 30 Administrative Officers (AOs) at the Naval Research Laboratory. These AOs and their COTRs are affiliated with the different divisions at the laboratory in order to test CESA for its coverage of a wide variety of procurement requests. As part of this group, there are very experienced COTRs in order to further check the validity of the knowledge in CESA. This wider testing occurred toward the beginning of the U.S. Government's fiscal year when there are many procurement request packages being generated by the COTRs for obtaining the future year's funding. This drove the use of CESA by the COTRs and ultimately generated more comments about CESA.

Based on the system's success, we are looking into developing the post-award phase component of CESA for future work. Additionally, we are exploring the use of hypertext for providing advice on completing selected pre-award procurement forms.

IMPLEMENTATION AND MAINTENANCE ISSUES

Even during the testing and evaluation phase of CESA, user training was an important component to help ensure that CESA was used. Training was provided to the users during a one and one-half hour session. In the first half-hour, a vugraph presentation on what an expert system is and how CESA was developed was given to the users. In the next 30 minutes, the knowledge engineer ran through a sample session of CESA showing most of the helpful features that the user might want to employ. The sample session was shown using a large projection screen. In the last 30 minutes, users could ask questions about CESA and even run through a sample session on their own. The users were provided with a run-time disk of CESA, an evaluation questionnaire, and a quick reference guide on how to use CESA. Figure A-8 shows the quick reference material on CESA. More elaborate documentation will be provided when CESA is finally transitioned into use at NRL.

Navy Center for Applied Research in AI
Code 5510
Naval Research Laboratory
Washington, D.C. 20375

1. For Inquiries and Comments, Contact: Laura C. Davis, Code 5510. Naval Research Laboratory or Jay Liebowitz, Code 5510.

2. Minimum Requirements: IBM PC, XT, AT or compatible; 640K RAM, Hard Disk or high density floppy disk drive, DOS 2.0 or higher, Exsys Professional runtime disks, and CESA disk.

3. CESA: CESA (COTR Expert System Aid) is an expert system prototype for helping the Acquisition Request Originator (ARO)/Contracting Officer Technical Representative (COTR) answer questions relating mostly to a contract's pre-award phase. In the past, the ARO/COTR has had difficulty in assembling complete Procurement Request (PR) packages and in keeping up-to-date with the many changing regulations in Contracts that affect the ARO/COTR. CESA is designed to help the ARO/COTR in the following major areas:

   • Aid in answering questions relating to the pre-award phase of a contract.
   • Aid in obtaining advice for completing selected pre-award forms and showing sample completions.
   • Help in obtaining information about selected post-award areas.

   CESA is just a prototype—it is not intended to be in its final delivery form. Your inputs will be extremely helpful in improving the accuracy and ease-of-use of CESA. Your comments will be incorporated into the next version of CESA.

4. What is EXSYS? CESA is built using Exsys Professional (hereafter called Exsys), a generalized expert system development package, popularly known as an expert system "shell." An expert system is an application of artificial intelligence; it is a computer program that acts like a human expert performing a

Figure A-8   Quick reference user documentation using CESA
via Exsys Professional

well-defined task [2]. Problem areas for which a person or group of persons with special expertise needed by others can be identified are possible candidates for expert system development. For example, an expert system has been built that helps customers to select personal computer hardware components from a bewildering list of products. Another expert system helps maintenance workers to identify problems with a piece of equipment [11].

An expert system "shell" package contains two main programs to let one:

1. Create an expert system (enter it into the computer). This function is performed by an expert system developer, usually called the knowledge engineer, or by an expert.

2. Run an expert system (anytime after it has been entered). This function is performed by a user.

When a user runs an expert system developed with Exsys, the system will begin by asking several questions relevant to the "problem domain." The user responds by selecting one or more answers from a list or by entering data. The computer continues to ask questions until it has reached a conclusion. The conclusion may be the selection of a single solution or a list of possible solutions arranged in order of likelihood. The computer can explain, in English, how it arrived at its conclusion and why. The final goal of an expert system is to select the most appropriate solution(s) to a problem based on the responses supplied by a user to the questions asked.

5. Expert System Development: Expert Systems can be developed for a problem that involves a selection from among a definable group of choices where the decision is based on logical rules [11]. The rules that the program uses are IF-THEN-ELSE type rules. A rule is made up of a list of IF conditions (normal English sentences or algebraic expressions) and lists of THEN and ELSE conditions (more sentences). If the computer determines that all of the IF conditions in a rule are true, it adds the rule's THEN conditions to what it knows to be true. If any of the IF conditions are false, the ELSE conditions are added to what is known.

Figure A-8   (continued)

The ability to derive information from rules allows the program to combine many small pieces of knowledge to arrive at logical conclusions about complex problems. A so-called "rule editor" allows the rules to be entered into Exsys. The rule editor also handles changes, additions, and deletions of rules.

Rules are stored in a file called the "knowledge base." A problem domain expert may be the developer of a knowledge base, or the expert may work with someone else to do the development work.

Others, called users, are expected to consult the expert system for advice. When others "run a consultation," Exsys uses its built-in "inference engine" program to process the knowledge base [11].

6. Important Points to Remember When Using Exsys
   - If you do not understand why a question is being asked, you can type

     w h y

   to see the rule that is being worked on.
   - If you are unsure of the meaning of a question, you can type

     ?

   to get a description. If there are no descriptions available, CESA will say "No explanation available."
   - If you want information about the post-award areas, you may get the message, "Conclusions are beyond the scope of CESA." This means that we have not built up that section of CESA.
   - If you make a mistake or want to change your answer to a question while running a user session with CESA, you can hit the

     CTRL and U keys (press the CTRL key and
     while holding it down, press the U key)

   Figure A-8   (continued)

to back up through a maximum of 10 previous questions to undo/redo your answers.

7. Getting Started. You should have three disks*: Exsys Professional Runtime Version, Exsys Professional Overlay, and the CESA disk. Load DOS into your computer. We will now copy the files on all the three floppy disks to your hard disk. Put your Exsys Professional Runtime disk in drive A and at the A⟩, type:

```
COPY *.* C:
```

Then put the Exsys Professional Overlay disk in drive A and at the A⟩, type:

```
COPY *.* C:
```

Next, put your CESA disk in drive A and at the A⟩, type

```
COPY *.* C:
```

After copying the files, you can now type:

```
EXSYSP CESA
```

to start your user session with CESA.

After loading Exsys and CESA, a screen will first appear indicating the Exsys Professional Runtime logo and then another screen will ask:

```
Do you wish instructions on running the
program (Y/N):

Answer Y if you want instructions or
answer N if you don't.
```

* If using double-density (i.e., low-density), you will have *three* disks. If using high density, you will have only *one* disk.

Figure A-8   (continued)

You will next be asked if you want the rules displayed during the run. Type N so that the program will run faster without displaying all the rules that are invoked during a sample run.

Next, the system will ask you if you want to recover previously saved input. Type: N for no.

Next, your user session will begin by showing you the title of the knowledge base and the authors. After you have read the title screen, press any key to continue.

You will then be shown general instructions on using CESA. Once the initial screens have been displayed, the program will start to execute the rules in CESA.

8. Sample Case: Suppose that you, as the ARO/COTR, are faced with the task of putting together a complete procurement request (PR) package. However, you are not sure which forms should be included in the package. Let's say that your PR involves a $150,000 procurement for an ADP-related research and development study; the procurement is a new research effort at NRL; procurement is competitive and there are companies related to the PR that are on the GSA schedule; there at least two offerors on the GSA schedule who can perform the work. The screens (see Figure A-1) show you a sample run of this scenario using CESA. The screens are annotated to provide you with additional comments.

Happy Contracting!

Figure A-8   (continued)

Since CESA is still a prototype, introduction and implementation of CESA into NRL has been deliberately gradual. Before we "broadcast" CESA to the NRL, the CESA knowledge engineering team wants to make sure that CESA is accurate and meets the needs of the users. Running historical test cases against CESA and having a staged approach to evaluating it have been useful ingredients to making sure CESA meets its intended goals. The staged approach consisted first of having a small test group work with CESA over a four-week period and then having about 30 Administrative Officers throughout NRL use CESA over one and one-half months. The Administrative Officers, who represent each Code at NRL, serve as another round of testing and evaluation before giving CESA to the 2,000 COTRs at NRL. By specifically targeting the Administrative Officers, word about CESA will likely spread throughout the laboratory, and hopefully this will set the stage for acceptance of CESA by the COTRs (although acceptance should be rather easy because the COTRs are in desperate need of aids to help them in their procurement process!). The comments from the Administrative Officers will then be incorporated into CESA and then CESA will be fielded to the COTRs throughout NRL.

Since there are so many COTRs at NRL, licensing was an important issue from the outset of the CESA project. Some shell vendors charge on a per-copy basis for multiple run-time copies of their shell. Since there are about 2,000 COTRs at NRL, a per-copy charge could be exorbitant. Thus, one of the criteria used in selecting an appropriate shell, if any, was the issue of a cost for run-time licenses. Exsys, Inc. charged a one-time price of under $1000 for a run-time license of Exsys Professional. This run-time license allowed multiple copies of the Exsys Professional Run-time program (and CESA) to be distributed to the COTRs at NRL. This non-commercial run-time license allowed the CESA knowledge engineering team to distribute CESA to an unlimited number of users at NRL on a noncommercial basis.

Besides licensing, another critical issue regarding the institutionalization of CESA at NRL is maintenance. In the contracting environment, as in the legal environment, rules and regulations change frequently. For CESA to be used, it was recognized at the beginning of the project that maintenance would play a key role. The Contracts Division at NRL, the sponsor of the project, also recognized the importance of maintaining and updating CESA. Contracts is in the process of putting an infrastructure in place within Contracts in order to maintain, update, and answer questions relating to CESA. This will most likely entail having one of the Contracts specialists, who is knowledgeable about computers, be assigned as part of his or her job duties to handle the maintenance of CESA. Of course, the AI Center at NRL would continue to be an outside advisor to provide help to this individual in maintaining and updating CESA. The CESA knowledge engineering team will groom this individual on how to work Exsys and modify CESA. One reason why Exsys was selected as the expert system shell for CESA was because of this very reason that it should be easy to learn and use. Because someone in Contracts is maintaining CESA, it was also recognized up front that CESA should be only a moderate-sized expert system and not be so unwieldy that it would be difficult to maintain.

CONCLUSIONS

CESA, from the initial comments from the users, is a helpful tool to the COTR in providing advice relating to the pre-award phase of a contract. One interesting occurrence from CESA's development was that CESA was a catalyst for stimulating policy changes in Contracts. If something was unclear and before that information was put in CESA, the expert would speak to the appropriate individuals within Contracts and NRL to clarify Contracts' policy on that issue. Oftentimes, this provoked policy changes which seemed to improve, in both understanding and content, Contracts policy.

REFERENCES

[1]   Liebowitz, J., L. C. Davis, and W. F. Harris, "CESA: An Expert
       System Prototype for Aiding U.S. Department of Defense Research
       Contracting," in *Expert Systems for Business and Management*, J. Lie-
       bowitz (ed.), Prentice Hall, Englewood Cliffs, NJ, 1990.

[2]   Liebowitz, J., *Introduction to Expert Systems*, Mitchell Publishing,
       Watsonville, CA, 1988.

[3]   Liebowitz, J. and D. A. DeSalvo (eds.), *Structuring Expert Systems:
       Domain, Design, and Development*, Yourdon Press/Prentice Hall, En-
       glewood Cliffs, NJ, 1989.

[4]   DeSalvo, D. A. and J. Liebowitz (eds.), *Managing AI and Expert
       Systems*, Prentice Hall, Englewood Cliffs, NJ, 1990.

[5]   Liebowitz, J., L. C. Davis, and W. F. Harris, "Using Expert Systems
       to Help the Contracting Officer Technical Representative: A Fea-
       sibility Study and Selection Methodology," *Educational Technology*,
       Educational Technology Publications, Englewood Cliffs, NJ, 1989.

[6]   Decision Support Software, Inc., *Expert Choice Manual*, McLean,
       Virginia, 1988.

[7]   Nazareth, D. L., "Issues in the Verification of Knowledge in Rule-

Based Systems," *International Journal of Man-Machine Studies*, Vol. 30, No. 3, Academic Press, New York, March 1989.

[8]   Harrison, P. R., "Testing and Evaluation of Knowledge-Based Systems," in *Structuring Expert Systems: Domain, Design, and Development*, J. Liebowitz and D. A. DeSalvo (eds.), Yourdon Press/Prentice Hall, Englewood Cliffs, NJ, 1989.

[9]   Jacobs, J. M. and C. W. J. Chee, "Specification of Expert Systems-Vol. III: Expert System Testing," TR88-303, Prepared for HQ Space Division, PO Box 92960, Los Angeles, CA 90009-2960, November 7, 1988.

[10]   Liebowitz, J., "Useful Approach for Evaluating Expert Systems," *Expert Systems*, Vol. 3, No. 2, Learned Information, Oxford, England, 1986.

[11]   Mockler, R. J. and D. G. Dologite, *Exsys: Expert System Tutorial*, Prentice Hall, Englewood Cliffs, NJ 1988.

INDEX